FOR ALL THE SAINTS

THE PRACTICE OF MINISTRY IN THE FAITH COMMUNITY

Edited by Melanie A. May

The Brethren Press, Elgin, IL

FOR ALL THE SAINTS
The Practice of Ministry in the Faith Community

Edited by Melanie A. May

Cover Design by Jeane Healy

The Brethren Press, Elgin, IL 60120

Library of Congress Cataloguing-in-Publication Data

For all the saints : the practice of ministry in the faith community / edited by Melanie A. May.

p. cm.

Includes bibliographical references.

ISBN 0-87178-292-8

1. Church of the Brethren--Clergy. 2. Pastoral theology--Church of the Brethren. I. May, Melanie A.

BX7826.F67 1990

253--dc20 90-42737

CIP

TABLE OF CONTENTS

CONTRIBUTORS

John J. Cassel is Dean of Students at Bethany Theological Seminary, Oak Brook, Illinois. He was co-coordinator of the Lilly Endowment grant jointly awarded to the Church of the Brethren General Board and Bethany Theological Seminary.

Robert E. Faus is Consultant for Ministry on the staff of the Church of the Brethren General Board, Elgin, Illinois. He is an active member of the National Council of Churches sub-unit on professional church leadership, and served on the coordinating committee for the Lilly Endowment grant.

Rosemary Haughton lives and works at Wellspring House, a shelter for the homeless that also administers a land trust for affordable housing, Gloucester, Massachusetts. A well-known writer and speaker, she is a Roman Catholic laywoman, mother of nine, and author of thirty-five books.

Melanie A. May is Ecumenical Officer and Executive of the Office of Human Resources of the Church of the Brethren General Board, Elgin, Illinois. She was co-coordinator of the Lilly Endowment grant, and is involved with the Faith and Order work of both National and World Councils of Churches.

Lauree Hersch Meyer is Associate Professor of Biblical Theology and Interpretation at Bethany Theological Seminary, Oak Brook, Illinois. She is an active member of the National Council of Churches' Working Group on Faith and Order, and served on the coordinating committee for the Lilly Endowment grant.

Sarah Baile Steele and Joyce Smit, Bethany staff persons, and Barbara A. Greenwald, of the Church of the Brethren General Board staff, contributed untold hours in support of the Lilly Endowment grant and in preparation of this manuscript.

INTRODUCTION

FOR ALL THE SAINTS: THE PRACTICE OF MINISTRY IN THE CHURCH

Melanie A. May

"Protestant, Roman Catholic and Jewish leaders alike are haunted by the challenge of maintaining the number and quality of their clergies despite the lure of much more lucrative professions and the exceptional demands of religious callings." So wrote Peter Steinfels of The New York Times in an article that made the front page headlines: "Shortage of Qualified New Clergy Causing Alarm for U.S. Religions."[1] "The spiritual life of the nation is at stake," says Rabbi Gary P. Zola, dean of admissions and student affairs at Hebrew Union College-Jewish Institute of Religion in the Steinfels' article. The matter of religious leadership should be "no less compelling for the society than questions about life expectancy or infant morality rates or illiteracy."[2]

Two years before the Steinfels' article appeared, the Indianapolis-based Lilly Endowment had published a paper in which it was suggested that the quality of persons studying at theological schools had slipped. "We've never touched a nerve so raw," said Fred L. Hofheinz, religion program director for the Lilly Endowment, "people told us we had dared to say what a lot of them were thinking but no one wanted to declare."[3] Shortly after publishing this paper, the Lilly Endowment announced a competitive grants program on "calling and forming quality ministerial candidates."

Over 200 proposals were submitted for the first of two tiers of grants to be awarded. This is one among many indicators that the matter of ministerial leadership is pressing for most churches and theological schools in the United States. A number of grants were awarded to Roman Catholic institutions. For Roman Catholics, the nation's largest religious denomination, the question of the future of the priesthood has reached crisis proportions. The Catholic population has grown steadily over the past 65 years, while the number of seminarians preparing for the priesthood has declined drastically, especially since 1966.[4] Moreover, there are estimates that about one-third of all priests ordained in the 1960's have resigned from the priesthood.[5] So serious is the shortage of Roman Catholic priests throughout the world that the synod of bishops meeting in Rome in September, 1990, will discuss the formation of priests.[6]

For the United Methodist Church, with 9 million members in the third largest denomination in the country, after the Catholics and the Southern Baptists, 42 percent of the active clergy will retire before 1995. The number of those preparing for ministry has declined annually for the last five years. The Presbyterian Church (U.S.A.), the Evangelical Lutheran Church in America, and the Christian Church (Disciples of Christ) face similar statistics. Each of these churches has launched major studies of ministry. These studies address not only concerns for the quality and quantity of future candidates for ministry, but also raise questions of the theology and practice of ministry, including questions of the orders of ministry.[7]

This decline in ministerial leadership is linked, at least in part, to the recent realignment of the religious landscape in the United States. Churches long referred to as "mainline" or "mainstream," meaning "the dominant, culturally established faiths held by the majority of Americans,"[8] have been losing membership as well as influence on the national scene. While most of the members lost are lost to the secular society rather than to other churches, the disestablishment of "mainline" churches has been accompanied by an assertion of power and prominence on the part of churches referred to as evangelical.[9]

But concerns about the quality and quantity of ministerial leadership for the future are perhaps more profoundly connected to two other factors. The first is that seminarians today are distinctly different from those of the recent past. According to the Steinfels' article:

> In the mid'1960's, 95 percent of protestant seminarians were male and their average age was 26. A quarter of a century later, the average age was up by almost 10 years and a third of those seeking ordination in mainline Protestant seminaries were women. . . . Virtually all seminary educators agree that the first large groups of women to enter seminaries in the 1970's were unusually capable and highly motivated. Only the influx of women has kept the shortage of talented seminarians from being much graver, the educators said.[10]

These older seminarians and particularly the women seminarians have raised questions about reigning perspectives on the practice of ministry. In a Lilly Endowment-funded study on women ministers, Barbara Brown Zikmund found that women are questioning the institution of ordained ministry itself. She quotes one woman who said: "When I was not ordained, I thought that I needed the recognition and authority [that ordination would bring], but now that I've got it, I question any ecclesiology or theology of ministry that needs it."[11] Zikmund goes on to say that "for many women today, the vocational crisis is not whether the church will ordain them, but whether they want to be ordained."[12] The status and shape of ordained ministry is beginning to change as more and more women who are ordained embody new ways of understanding and practicing their ministries.[13]

A second factor affecting the shortage of quality ministerial leadership in the United States today is, I believe, the professionalization of the practice of ministry. The concern for ministry's professionalization is among the hottest topics being discussed in church and seminary circles. Perspectives on professionalization are deeply divergent. On one hand, Leonard Sweet argues:

> "Professionalism" has led us to the point where the central motivating symbol of ministry is the ladder, rather than the cross. . . . We glory in the cross of Christ, not the ladder of success, a ladder kicked away forever when Jesus slipped on the Via Dolorosa. . . . The word "profession" itself, which once entailed notions of ecclesial responsibility and public values, has now come to mean little more than "expert-for-hire."[14]

Sweet's perspective is akin to the one articulated by Roger Finke and Rodney Stark who correlate the decline of church life with the move to a ministry practiced by the professionally trained and suggest that, already in colonial times, reliance on a professional ministry created a practical problem: "a constant shortage of clergy."[15] On the other hand, there are those for whom the word "professional" translates as "well-trained." A recent study reveals that laity prefer pastors who are professionals in this sense, but they assume these pastoral professionals also identify themselves as servants.[16]

This book is a case study set amid these contemporary circumstances. The Church of the Brethren, while not classified as a "mainline" church, at least according to the typology of Roof and McKinney, has nonetheless been faced with loss of membership and a shortage of quality ministerial leadership. Even before the Lilly Endowment announced the 1987 Competitive Grant, the Church of the Brethren General Board together with Bethany Theological Seminary had convened a committee on calling to consider these matters of ministry. When the Competitive Grant on calling and forming quality ministerial candidates was announced, therefore, the groundwork for writing a proposal had been done. The grant proposal jointly-submitted by the General Board and Bethany Theological Seminary was one of 40 out of 200 awarded funds in the first tier of grant competition.

The usefulness of a case study depends, in part, upon clearly setting forth the particularities of the case considered. This clarity enables others to identify with the particulars of the case or to distinguish the uniqueness of their own circumstances. What follows is a sketch of the Church of the Brethren, cast to be relevant to the matters of ministry at hand.

The Church of the Brethren was founded in eighteenth-century Germany by a group of people profoundly influenced by sixteenth-century Anabaptism and by the Radical Pietist stream running around them. From the beginning, Brethren have understood the church to be not a voluntary association of like-minded believers but a close-knit community whose life together is a means of grace. Neither a creed, nor a liturgy, nor an official hierarchy, nor a building makes the church to be the church. The church is made visible wherever and whenever members come together for worship and work dedicated to God.[17]

Brethren have stressed obedience to the teachings of Jesus and conformity to the life of early Christian communities. Turning to the New Testament as its only creed, Brethren have practiced believers' baptism by trine immersion, feetwashing at the Lord's Supper according to John 13, the holy kiss, anointing the sick, reconciliation of conflict according to Matthew 18, simplicity of life, and nonresistance. These practices have led Brethren, particularly in the twentieth-century, into service, peacemaking and ecumenical engagement beyond the boundaries of the community.

But the Brethren have not been culturally established. During the early eighteenth-century in Germany, the illegal status of the newly-baptized group of believers led to their immigration to Pennsylvannia. During the Revolutionary War, Brethren refused to fight and were, therefore, thought to be traitors or Loyalists. Brethren were shunned, fined, and imprisoned. During the Civil War, particularly in the South, Brethren were once again cast out because of the refusal to bear arms. Many Brethren, consequently, were convinced that obedience to the teachings of Jesus is possible only when protected by nonconformity in relation to the surrounding culture.

Since the earliest Brethren beginnings, the affirmation of the "priesthood of all believers" has been clearly articulated. Brethren have said that to be baptized is to be ordained to ministry, this is to say, to the ministry of the whole church. Indeed, the Church of the Brethren was founded by laity. Alexander Mack, the founder, acted in the role of elder or minister, but there is no record of whether or when he was "ordained." All members, irrespective of their role in the congregation, were addressed simply as "sister" or "brother."

Only gradually did Brethren begin to speak about persons who practiced various particular sorts of ministry with terms that were more formal than functional. For example, in an earlier era, the persons who were primarily responsible for the annual visit to every home in the congregation were spoken of a "visiting Brethren." Today we speak of such persons as deacons, a word with a somewhat more formal and official flavor. Similarly, in an earlier era, members of the congregation were free to stand and speak. The congregation would choose from among these speakers who should be chosen for particular ministerial responsibilities. Those chosen were referred to as the ones "set forward," a literal description of the way in which those chosen to preach were set forward to sit behind the table with other ministers who faced the deacons sitting on the other side of the table. Those who assumed these degrees of ministry were frequently referred to as housekeepers or householders to describe their role as that of overseer.[18]

By the nineteenth-century a threefold ministry had evolved alongside the office of deacon. There were "ministers on trial," (first degree, currently known as licensed ministers), speakers or exhorters called ministers (second degree, currently known as ordained ministers), and elders so designated because of special maturity and standing in the life of the community (third degree, which was eliminated in the 1960's). Persons in the third degree of ministry were sometimes also called the bishop. All these ministers, including the deacons, were called by the congregation. None of these ministers was salaried. None was formally trained or educated. None was formally set apart as different in kind.

It is clear that in the nineteenth-century the Brethren excluded women from calling or election to these ministerial offices as well as from the office of deacon on scriptural and traditional grounds. There is, however, some evidence that suggests women were not so excluded in an earlier era. Although there is no record that specifies responsibilities, Alexander Mack, Jr. refers to three women as elders in his list of deaths.[19] Despite their official exclusion, there were women who preached during the nineteenth-century. Foremost among these pioneering women were Sarah Righter Major and Mattie Cunningham Dolby, the first woman whose name appeared on the ministerial list of the Church of the Brethren.[20] In response to this practice and the controversy surrounding it, the 1922 Annual Meeting, the body with highest legislative authority for the Church of the Brethren, provided for "licensing sisters to preach."[21] For men, licensing was the first step toward ordination to the full ministry. For women, the license to preach was a permanent license without the possibility of ordination. The 1958 Annual Conference finally granted women "full and unrestricted rights in the ministry."[22]

As noted above, the original pattern for ministry was unsalaried or "free" ministry. Those called or elected by the congregation as ministers were most often farmers or teachers. They earned their living independently while serving in a set-apart ministry. The first record of a full-time salaried pastor is in 1891. By World War II, two-thirds of the congregations in the Church of the Brethren had salaried pastors. The move from "free" ministry, which was also a plural ministry insofar as more than one minister served in a congregation, to salaried pastoral ministry was rapid and rather unreflective.

Robert E. Faus, who was in conversation with 210 persons in twenty-two congregations regarding this transition, reports hearing about "a rising dissatisfaction with an existing ministry rather than anticipation and excitement about the prospects of salaried pastoral ministry."[23] Faus specifies this "rising dissatisfaction" with reference to shifts in employment patterns among the Brethren, reflecting wider societal shifts:

> Farmer-preachers or teacher-preachers were being replaced by persons employed as hourly wage-earners, professionals with demands on their time or self-employed business persons, all of whom found less freedom for day-to-day visitation, funerals or emergency ministry. There was pressure for more church programming, more work youth and young adults, and better preaching.
>
> A net effect of these developments was the recognition that "the old ways" . . . were not quite adequate. This was often acknowledged by the free ministers themselves.[24]

Other changes--the move to elected church boards, formal church budgets, new church buildings, revised constitutions, along with the discontinuation of the annual visit--indicate that the transition from "free" to salaried ministry accompanied or was accompanied by greater attention to church organization.[25]

Salaried pastoral ministry, for which professional training was increasingly considered necessary, has characterized the understanding and practice of ministry in the Church of the Brethren, at least since the 1940's. During the last twenty years, however, two programs of ministry training have arisen that recover the pattern of "free" ministry for today. Education for a Shared Ministry (EFSM) locates ministry training in the congregational setting, and engages congregational members along with the person called into set-apart ministry in a particular congregation. Training in Ministry (TRIM) is a program for persons called into church leadership who wish to continue their education to prepare for service as set-apart ministers in the whole church.

Even with three tracks for ministry training--Education for a Shared Ministry, Training in Ministry, and seminary degree--some small Church of the Brethren congregations are served by persons who neither have adequate pastoral training nor know the Church of the Brethren. This problem is particularly serious since the Church of the Brethren is a denomination of small congregations. More than half of the one thousand congregations have too few financial and human resources to support a full-time professionally trained pastor. These congregations nonetheless think that to have pastoral ministry they must have a full-time, professionally trained person. Compounded by the fact that fewer Church of the Brethren candidates for ministry are graduating from seminaries, pressure to "fill the pulpit" takes precedence over quality ministry.

Even for the congregations able to support a full-time, professionally trained pastor, the future is in the balance. In 1988, Bethany Theological Seminary graduated seven candidates for ministry, not half of the fifteen needed annually to fill the available positions. The dearth of well-trained candidates will become more pronounced as the Church of the Brethren, along with other denominations, faces the retirement of pastoral ministers at a extraordinary rate during the 1990's.

Against the background of Church of the Brethren experience in ministry and the backdrop of this sort of analysis, the General Board and Bethany Theological Seminary set forth the following goals and objectives for the grant process:

a. To assess congregational initiative and involvement in calling as a primary asset in recruiting and selecting candidates for ministry.

b. To assess denominational connectedness and support structures which enable and undergird congregational recruitment efforts.

c. To promote denominational program development in support of persons moving toward set-apart leadership within this understanding of ministry.

d. To articulate and promote a particular theological understanding of "ministry with" which grows out of the Believers' Church heritage and to draw out its implications for leadership development.

The process of articulating a particular understanding of ministry began with the Eighth Believers' Church Conference on ministry, held at Bethany Theological Seminary, September 2-5, 1987.[26] This process continued on the basis of a draft statement, "Theological Reflections on Ministry in the Church of the Brethren," prepared by Melanie A. May for discussion at a series of colloquies convened to consider recruitment of ministerial candidates. These colloquies also discussed data from a survey of congregations regarding their understanding and experience of calling persons to ministry, carried out by Robert E. Faus, along with data from interviews of ordained ministers regarding their experiences of being called and formed for ministry, conducted by John J. Cassel. Final drafts of these documents are chapters three, four, and five in this book. The conversation at these colloquies surfaced and clarified five themes: calling; forming; training and support; quality; and spirituality. Chapter one in this book is a summary of the conversation around these themes prepared by Lauree Hersch Meyer.

Of the five themes, the one that surprised the planner was spirituality. In response to this concern that arose out of conversation, Rosemary Haughton, well-known Roman Catholic lay theologian,[27] was invited to speak to a spirituality of ministry at the leadership conference culminating the Lilly grant process in December, 1989. Chapter two is an edited transcription of her talks, which were given in the context of worship at the conference. Remarkably, the spirituality she sets forth, which is very practical as well as sacramental in its sensibility, resonates deeply with traditional Brethren themes of service and simple living as signs of the presence of God among the people now, and recasts these themes for the wider church of Jesus Christ.

The stuff of this case study is for all faithful followers of Jesus Christ--for all the saints--who seek words that bear witness to a way ahead in the church's ministry. There are, of course, no readily available answers to the problems the churches in the United States face now and for the future. There is, however, hope inasmuch as we engage one another in conversation that is genuine and gracious. There is hope as we begin wherever we are ourselves engaged in ministry to embody newness. In this hope of the Word become flesh and to this end this case study is offered.

CHAPTER ONE

A CALL TO CONVERSATION: MINISTERIAL LEADERSHIP IN THE CHURCH OF THE BRETHREN

Lauree Hersch Meyer

In December 1988, and February 1989, the Church of the Brethren General Board and Bethany Theological Seminary with funding from the Lilly Foundation, coordinated a series of colloquies to discuss calling and forming of quality ministerial leadership in the Church of the Brethren. Five themes emerged as central to these conversations: calling, formation, training and support, quality, and spirituality.

What follows is a focused summary of each theme, a series of questions to spark conversation in various gatherings of persons concerned about ministry and calling. Along with reflections on each theme emerging from the colloquy conversations.

Calling

> **Congregational initiative in calling is a compelling matter for the Church of the Brethren. Our understanding of church locates the responsibility for calling to ministry leadership in the local worshipping community. This raises the question of how congregations as communities of worship and lived faith best nurture patterns and practices that result in naming and commissioning members whose gifts will lead the church into its ministry.**

The church is both a called and a calling body. A congregation's sense of its mission and call is directly related to how the congregation takes initiative in calling its members to ministry, and whom, how, and to what ministry it calls people. When a church views ministry as something someone does in and for the congregation rather than as the whole church's vocation, its vision limits the church's ability to call all members into ministry, except as all are asked to contribute to the church's program. When a church views ministry as a commitment made and an ordination received in baptism to serve God throughout God's whole world, congregations may ask how each member is called to ministry and mission as a member of Christ's risen and living body.

Clarity about how each of us is called to minister helps us identify what specific (or set-apart) leadership we need in order to nurture, train, and support our congregational ministries. Knowing what leadership we seek and why we need it, contributes to church people cherishing their leaders.

The ministry to which the Church of the Brethren calls and is called, is ministry with, not for, others,[1] whether we speak of the ministry of each in daily life or of the ministries of set-apart church leaders. We understand God's incarnate presence in Jesus Christ through the Holy Spirit as diakonia **with** humankind.[2] Jesus life in ministry was "in every way" like that of the people he called to fullness of life and to become a serving community, a communion of saints who bless one another and praise God. We who are made in God's image may also live in God's image: as members of Christ called to a mutual ministry that upbuilds Christ's body and the communion of saints all of whom serve together.

When we speak of the ministry to which each member as well as set-apart leaders are called, we are therefore guided not first and foremost by "objective" job-descriptions. We primarily consider the "fit" between the person and the particular ministry, which we find as important as a persons's knowledge, skills, and spirit. When the ministries of all church members and those of its set-apart leaders "match," ordained ministers will serve in places where the gifts and needs of a congregation and those of its set-apart leaders mutually enhance and support one another.

People were "elected" rather than "called" into the set-apart ministry before the salaried professional ministry was predominant in the Church of the Brethren. Congregations then used the word election much as we use the word calling today. Both words speak to the way in which leadership fits the church's ministry vision. An important difference between election and calling to ministry is that in the unsalaried or "free" ministry persons were elected to serve the same group that empowered them, while those called into the church's set-apart ministry today rarely serve the churches that call them. Social and contextual implications, as well as theological values, are communicated by both words. "Calling" has come to imply a democratic and "election" a more republicalor representational model of church authority. This difference accurately reflects social changes between this and earlier generations, changes keenly felt by some members and visible in most of our churches.

In more recent years, most people come into leadership in the Church of the Brethren through their own initiative. The need to take personal initiative or "sell oneself" in order to enter the church's set-apart ministry further reflects the church's tendency to practice contemporary cultural values and procedures, while continuing to proclaim more familiar traditional and biblical-theological values. This duplicity is confusing and problematic. Sisters and brothers from cultures whose leadership expectations resemble the church of several decades ago, are amazed to see Anglos putting themselves forward for leadership. In their country, as earlier in the Church of the Brethren, self-selection is a kiss of death for future leadership. We know the church's **spirit** is always God's Holy Spirit known in Christ Jesus; we also know the church's **shape** appropriately reflects the form or shape of its culture. Those of us who live in North American Anglo culture can expect self-selection to remain one way by which persons come into leadership and set-apart ministry in the Church of the Brethren.

Whatever the values, even necessities, of any cultural pattern, each also has difficulties. One difficulty the Church of the Brethren has shown in responding to self-selected leadership is members' inability to say "no" both honestly and compassionately to persons who seek set-apart leadership, but whose personal needs get in the way of their ability to serve. When the church affirms self-selected calls for the sake of meeting the persons' own needs, the result is not ministry.

Questions about calling and self-selection are particularly important in relation to the present open search process used to secure leadership for most of the church's institutions. If election and calling relate strongly to different social contexts, both the sociocultural and theological differences between the open search and call processes are also visible. The open search fits a community who does not know or think of all who are able and willing to serve within it. Theologically, the search implies that those chosen as leaders will shape and be shaped by the mutual work of ministry. The call fits communities who know persons available for ministry and who is itself of one mind. Theologically, the call assumes that those chosen to be leaders can step into the vacant "place" with relatively little adjustment on the part of either leader or people. In Church of the Brethren culture, it is appropriate to use both the search and the call, since church members are familiar with and value calling persons with particular gifts for ministry, but neither know nor know of many able persons with leadership ability who respond to an open search.

The process of securing a pastor in the Church of the Brethren has undergone major changes in the last century, moving from the unsalaried or "free" ministry model, in which members called from their midst into leadership persons who were already well-known, tested leaders to the salaried professional ministry model in which members (usually) call from outside their midst a (usually) professionally trained pastor to serve them, to a tendency sometimes present today to let the district executive secure a pastor for them.

The Church of the Brethren needs to review and reshape the placement process in ways that educate and encourage local churches to be thoughtful and responsible for taking initiative again for calling at all levels: calling each of its members into the church's whole ministry; laying hands on persons for set-apart leadership in its own and the wider church's ministry; securing able pastoral leadership to fit the congregation's situation and ministry; and challenging able, qualified persons in its midst to enter the church's professional leadership.

We are concerned that the social and cultural patterns that (often rightly) influence how we call persons into leadership also influence the values informing how we understand the church's ministry and leadership. For example, we sense that the spirituality of service often seems less central than our concern for achievement and recognition. We sometimes hesitate to call persons into leadership, for fear we might interfere with their lives. Local church needs often seem unimportant to members so that, for example, if asked to plan and tell a children's story, they regularly respond that they are "too busy:" with the result that few folks want to call them to a more demanding set-apart leadership in the church's life.

<u>The connection and accountability between the local call to licensed ministry and the district confirmation into the church's ordained ministry is weak</u>.[3] We believe changing social and cultural factors to which we have not made adequate responses help account for the weak connections and call us to imagine responses more adequate to our contexts. We have already noted the change from the unsalaried to the salaried ministry and the shift from congregational election or call to the self-selection process for calling out leaders. Several other phenomena also call for attention. In recent decades, most youth "leave home" for college or a job at about age 18. This is before they are well known personally to adult members of the congregation; moreover, they are usually both more deeply integrated into lives of, and concerned for approval from, their youthful peers than adults in the congregation.

Many of us suffer from confusing the affirmation of a specific call to service with personal affirmation. This confusion is visible in several practices that undermine the church's understanding of the call. One is that we select many of our leaders by "objective" performance measures, only to discern later that the fit between minister and people is not an adequate fit in this job at this place and in this time. An equally unhealthy counter-dependency emerges from our confusion between responding to peoples' need to be needed and calling people to the ministry that now fits for them. Our inability to speak honestly leads to confusion and anger when people feel called to the set-apart ministry or to candidate in an open search process. When we uncritically affirm or reject the call of people we doubt are pastoral material, or when we support or turn down people for jobs in response to their ability, hopes, needs, affability, sincerity, or commitment, we pay less attention to the "fit" that makes ministry work than to the person. But ministry is not for the minister. Ministry is service to God for the renewal of all God's people and the whole created universe.

The accountability and continuity between local mentoring in ministry and district discernment of the call to the church's ordained ministry is strengthened when leaders throughout the church deepen their spiritual life and see the nurture of each member's and the church's spiritual life as the center of all Christian life: the spirit that is the foundation for all ministry in Christ's name. One of our most basic needs is spiritual discipline that will sensitize us to God's Spirit so that we serve God, even when the situation or context is new or frightening or frankly offensive. As the church's understanding of each member's call to ministry influences how we call out members to the set-apart ministry, so the spirituality of our leaders influences the spirituality, as well as the biblical and theological depth, of the whole church and its members.

We note with interest that several decades ago, the concern for quality leadership focused on **retaining** ministers, while today we are concerned for calling and forming people for the set-apart ministry. In short we are concerned with making rather than keeping ministry attractive.[4] We are unsure whether this change in emphasis reflects the changed cultural situation in which we live, our acceptance of rapid job change in all vocations, a decline in the number and/or quality of persons training for the salaried ministry, a general decline in the church's spirituality in the wake of greater emphasis on church management and structure, more trust in new forms of ministry (second career, Education For a Shared Ministry, Training in Ministry, bi-vocational ministries), some combination of these, or yet other factors we have not noticed.

We hear of a leadership crisis in the church, but we are not clear what this means. Whose leadership crisis is it? Not all of us experience a leadership crisis. Perhaps the language of leadership crisis itself reflects changing patterns and conflicting perspectives among church members of different ages, genders, and social strata, as well as among local, district, and national church bodies and institutions. There is a vast pool of persons who have not traditionally been in leadership who are eager to be called into set-apart ministry--women, people of color, and ethnic people--even though the pool of traditional faces, white and male, is smaller. We are not sure if Anglo church members are willing to accept "others" as leaders. Inasmuch as we do not accept "others", we create the leadership crisis. When we ask how **we** may help, empower, and guide **them**, our paternalistic posture still robs us of the unique richness of gifts for leadership they may offer. We need to receive as well as give help, empowerment, and guidance in order to know the fullness of unity and communion as a people of God in ministry.

We also wonder how much what we call a leadership crisis results from our own values, reflecting the tendency in our world that places highest value on economic success and on upwardly-mobile professional placement, that find vocational ecclesial leadership less desirable. As structural, managerial, and economic values become norms basic for decision-making in matters of church leadership, policy, and program, these functional factors set the terms for and effectively replace the church's own vision, values, and theology.[5] Where formerly church and cultural leaders both relied on establishing leadership through relations with constituents, corporate leaders now have become used to setting the terms for decision-making. Therefore, where church leaders expect acceptance of their leadership because of their office, they often find themselves left with a vacuum without the expected swell of response. Accordingly, the culture-wide debunking of charismatic leadership among people of position often corresponds with this tendency to rely on office rather than relationship for authority in leadership.

We are all shaped by the context and content of our culture and our faith as we come to church membership and leadership. In a world where many of us have come to resist challenge to our "place" in familiar social structures and cultural expectations, God has blessed us with sisters and brothers from varied social contexts with diverse cultural expectations. These sisters and brothers are calling Christians to distinguish anew between cultural forms and the life of faith as we seek quality ministerial leadership in a world whose shape is in flux.

o What does calling mean to you? Obtaining pastoral leadership? Calling persons to set-apart ministry? Calling each Christian to service fitting for their talents and in fulfillment of their baptismal vows?

o Are all baptized members of Christ's risen, living body called into "priestly" ministry in the world? Who was called to what in scripture?

o Do you think of ministry more as a helping or a status profession?

o Is the salaried ministry a calling? If so, what distinguishes it as such? If not, how does the call relate to ministry?

o Are Christians "called" into vocations other than professional, salaried ministry? For example, are Christians called to be physicians, lawyers, farmers, businesspersons, teachers, social workers? Are these vocations also ministries? In what way?

o Do you value the set-apart ministry? Is it a vocation you desire for your children?

o When did you last challenge someone to enter a fulltime Christian vocation? How do you respond to people who consult with you about going into a fulltime Christian vocation?

o What impression do your children or friends get from the conversation around the Sunday lunch table about how ministry matters?

o What vocational profile do you cherish for your church's children and for the youth you love most?

Formation

It is clear from our research and conversations that formation is important because the sense of being called seldom comes as a one-time event. Since a variety of events usually influence us over a period of time, we need to focus on matters of formation in a new way. While Brethren have tended to think of transformation as the avenue to ministry, in our time we are called to attend to what happens at each stage of Christian development, and recognize how each is integral to formation for ministry.

"Formation"is a new word in Church of the Brethren our vocabulary, though we have long recognized how important it is to shape the whole lives of each member: hearts, minds, and spirits. In an earlier age, people knew all of their neighbors and few people moved from where they grew up, families knew one another intimately. In such a situation, we were "formed" as Brethren in our social sub-culture with no need to wonder about **how** to form a new generation. "It worked," and we let it go at that. One indication of how well it worked was that Brethren church leaders were often the leaders to whom people in the neighborhood looked for guidance as well. In this context, being a minister usually meant having the maturity and wisdom of judgment expected for leadership and respected among neighbors and townspeople who were not part of one's church.

The Brethren understanding of the set-apart ministry, as the ministry understanding of other churches, assumes the fullness of adulthood. When we speak of baptism as ordination into the "priesthood of all believers" or the whole church's ministry, we nevertheless assume that anyone called to exercise leadership in the church is formed, tested, and mature in her or his faith. To be called into the "set-apart" ministry presupposed a tested formation both in the faith and as a leader.

As long as the social structures of our life together "formed" us, we did not ask how to "form" identity as Christians and as members of the Church of the Brethren. But the context of our lives has changed. Most of us are not particularly close to our neighbors. Most of our neighbors are not Brethren. Many of our closest friends are neither Brethren nor neighbors. The business values and norms to which we refer in day-to-day decision-making, like the colleagues with whom we work, rarely help form our Christian, let alone our Brethren, identity.

In our changed context, we need to "do" formation more consciously, especially if we hope to resist being shaped by the strong non-Christian formation that influences our daily lives. From churches such as the Orthodox and the Roman Catholic, who have always viewed formation as a life-long process for Christians who are pilgrims, we seek the ecumenical gift of learning to form persons' Christian identity throughout their lives, so that baptism may indeed be ordination as a servant/minister in Christ's church.

Our congregational church experience where we grew up, forms our understanding of church. The local congregation's power as church forms each person nurtured in its midst, shaping how those who are touched by its life understand what church **is**: what constitutes the church's "normal" and normative ministry and mission. Given the church's vast and inescapable power to form the next generation, each church is called to nurture the next generation so that persons' formative experiences elicit trust and loyalty to God, love for the church, and passion to serve God in the world.

What we presuppose or assume about what it means to be church and about the shape of church life reflects early experiences that shaped our understandings. Not only our values are "formed" by our early experiences. The social reality we consider normative often bears the image of our early years. Whether we cherish, dislike, or disagree with what we knew in our formative years, our early experience of what is normal translates into a "normative" claim upon our adult understandings and expectations. Our automatic or thought-less childhood sense of what is normal about church does not distinguish between content and context. Thus, as adults, the content with which we think of church is often firmly rooted in the world of our formation, though we have located our professional and family life in a radically different context.

<u>Formation flourishes on repeated actions</u>: rites and rituals whose meaning impresses itself upon us in the drama of repetition. Brethren were born in a more rational age than the liturgical age of the ancient church. Consciously resisting the old church's liturgical drama, early Brethren drama and ritual related to Matthew 18 and the deacon's visit, and to John 13 and the Love Feast. These rites that have bound us emotionally to the events of God's incarnate presence among us were embodied in our life as a covenant community.

Now that the strong social formation of earlier generations is absent, our corporate identity as church seems weaker and our participation in these rites is less frequent. Indeed, the absence of our earlier formation is visible as current generations, unlike those of our forebearers, find it difficult to express our identity. It is not easy for most Brethren to say clearly who we are, what we believe, why we believe what we believe, and what it means for us to be Brethren.

As Allen Bloom states in <u>The Closing of the American Mind</u>, students today come to all institutions of learning far less formed as persons than in former generations.[6] This means institutions receiving persons for education will shape them in arenas once thought to be held for privileged parental perogative, in addition to forming them for professional, managerial, academic, and other "marketable skills." We also see this trend in seminaries, which now often receive persons for ministry training who have no experience in congregational life, who do not know scripture, who have not read the literature of theology, history, philosophy or the interpersonal and human sciences, and who have not learned to assess their own limits as well as assets. Faith formation is now as basic a priority for seminary education as information-sharing and skills-training. But it is difficult for the same seminary curriculum to provide adequate ministry training when it must also work at Christian faith formation. Perhaps the increasingly long wish list churches press upon seminaries reflects the reality that three years of seminary training are not adequate for ministry training unless students come well grounded in the church's faith and practice and in spiritual discipline.

Since seminary training intends that its graduates may be **recognized** as ministers, we ask what formation training contributes to persons' ability to nurture others in Christian faith and practice. This question is familiar both to the traditional Brethren unsalaried or "free" ministry formation and also to what Bishop Anthony Bloom of the Russian Orthodox Church practices when training priests. Bloom yokes a young man (all Orthodox priests are men) who feels called to be ordained with an excellent priest to work alongside in the parish as a mentor. The young man reports regularly to the bishop, who is his supervisor and has the authority to recommend him for ordination. Bloom lets the minister-in-training work alongside a seasoned priest until the people of the congregation approach him as bishop and ask that the young man be "priested," thereby affirming his service to them as a priest. Bishop Anthony finds that when a church asks for a person who has ministered to **them** to be ordained, the person is usually spiritually ready to live as a priest and usually has attained the necessary knowledge of polity, liturgy, and other practical matters.

While a priest is expected to study history, theology, liturgy, and scripture as a part of each day's discipline, Bishop Anthony does not consider formal seminary education or a degree to be essential to being a priest. He does, however, think it is fundamental for the church's life and faith. So when a priest comes to the bishop with questions that evidence his readiness and energy for more structured study, the priest is sent to seminary.

<u>Congregations influence the quality of ministers who go to the seminary for training</u>, which in turn effects the quality of ministry leadership that emerges from seminary education. Long-term involvement with others is basic to a strong faith formation. Short-term experiences with little relational reinforcement "form" people in ways very different from engaged interest in a person's identity. Since we believe that all church members are together responsible for formation, we reflected on how local congregations can intentionally strengthen the formation of all members throughout their lives for the sake of their ministries.

We believe it is important to begin by engaging the whole church in conversation about calling and training for ministry. In these colloquies, we have been energized. Our imagination and passion have been ignited through conversation founded in mutual commitment. We expect that others who invest themselves, with an eye to what they can do together and to what each can do in his or her own place, will experience a similar creative and energizing effect. We also encourage local churches to call for conversation with other local churches or for conversation at the district level.

In addition to conversing, each of us can intentionally plan to do more **mutual** ministry. Members, deacons, and ministry committee members from local churches may "adopt" younger folks in the congregation, showing interest in them and in "what you'll do when you grow up." When these folks become youth, members can stay in touch with what motivates and interests them, lifting up ministry in conversation with them and identifying what they already do or would like to do that is ministry both in their daily life and in the context of the church. When they leave for college or a job or volunteer service, we can remain in touch with our "adopted" family members. We can continue to show the kind of interest by which lives become bonded in deeper friendship and mutual identity so that as adults of various ages we can consider together how our faith is challenged by our experiences in the world of which we are part.

We can also intentionally mentor others in a mutual teaching-learning relationship in ministry. Much of what members do both "in" and "as" church lends itself to mentoring. One model of mentoring is to invite others to come with us when we visit people or undertake projects. By talking and praying about the event beforehand, as well as by reflecting on and praying about the people, the event, and our experience afterward, we open a window to the practice of ministry. Another way to mentor is to talk with our parents or children or to those of another generation about our vision for the church and about the ways we seek to embody our faith. Likewise, we may offer to give leadership or take part in events similar to those that have been most meaningful to us: work camps, summer camps, district or national conferences, youth or women's or young adult conferences.

Mentoring within and among church members and friends is an "on purpose" way to replace the formation that seems to have "automatically" taken place in our earlier, more geographically "stable" experience as a church. For example, in the 1940s and 1950s, a variety of activities helped mentor and form Brethren youth and young adult identity. During the 1960s and 1970s, Brethren camps, colleges and national youth conferences were the mentoring and "feeder" systems augmenting local congregational formation of youth toward active interest in lay and ordained ministries. In the 1980s, and as we enter the 1990s, many Brethren youth no longer choose Church of the Brethren colleges for their education. The small number of Brethren youth at Brethren colleges reduces the colleges influence as feeder systems for continuing to form persons for church leadership after youth leave the congregation of their early formation. Consequently, Brethren youth and young adults, who are enormously open to having their energy engaged and their identity shaped, are significantly influenced by other persons and perspectives.

Traditionally, most calling and formation structures of the Church of the Brethren have relied on the thick personal engagement among members to move people into the set-apart ministry. Whether we dislike or fail to notice it, our interpersonal connections in the church are far looser than they were only a few decades ago. We respond to culturally predominant professional and economic values. We are exposed to and saturated by the public media. We are not altogether clear how profoundly the technologically-oriented and consumerist society effects us, our congregational life, our understanding and practice of ministry. We need to become aware of and honest about how the values and influences of our sociocultural context shape us.

It often seems difficult for adults in the church to locate "where" Brethren youth are today. Do they feel commitment or indifference or irritation toward the church? Can we, in the absence of feeder systems into richer participation in the church's life when they complete high school, develop connections and keep in touch with youth as they become young adult professionals? Do we treasure our legacy enough to continue to nurture our heirs who we formed to know themselves as God's beloved children, disciplining ourselves with them to minister as faithful, responsible disciples, growing into maturity of mind and spirit that equips them for the church's set-apart ministry? We must find ways to keep in close touch with youth and young adults in the now scattered social structures in which they and, since the 1950s, many professionals who grew up and still think of themselves as Brethren, live.

Studies show that, as corporate bodies, congregations and denominations have certain "life-cycle" tendencies.[7] This is to say, as individual persons grow or fail to mature from the promise of infancy into eager childhood, sturdy adolescence, vigorous young adulthood, established adulthood, wise older adulthood, and eventual decline, so congregations may resemble these "stages" in their lives. Current studies describe characteristics of congregations at these different stages with little evidence about what makes and keeps churches spiritually healthy. The least we can say is that a healthy church lives its call from generation to generation, embodying its mission and ministry in daily life whatever the time or the place in which members find themselves. God's Holy Spirit at work in the church, enlivens persons in each local, district, national, or international church, even as each church is itself re-shaped by the changing sociocultural contexts of its members in their time and place. This returns us to the questions about where our youth are and about what our connections are to youth, young adults, as well as young and more mature professionals who grew up Brethren but who no longer live where they are active members of a congregation.

What is sometimes called a "shrinking pool of leaders," seems also to be reflective of a large group of youth, young adults, adults, and now older adults with strong early Brethren formation who were led to jobs in places where the denomination is not institutionally present. Yet the values and daily ministries of these "pilgrims" deeply resemble those of church members active in local congregations: business people, shop and union workers, teachers, social work and other professionals. The church has formed and nurtured little contact with these persons, though we could view and commission them as ministers in our mission outreach rather than as members now "lost" to existing church institutions. Indeed, we have found that when we have kept in contact with such persons, when we have them called to specific ministries in and for the church, they often respond positively and accept significant salary cuts to enter the church's set-apart ministry.

We may need a national strategy to devise connective structures that build upon local church early formation structures. But the focus of our discussion centered on what we who are involved in the church's many centers of life can do at local, district, (some) regional, and national levels. As members of local congregations who see our heirs move away from communities of formation, nurture, and support, each of us is called to devise whatever diverse and practical ways we can imagine so we remain connected with our "next generation." This challenge is particularly acute since for many youth graduation from high school is graduation from the church.

"Incarnation" is the theological name for the church's challenge to be and continue to be connected with each new generation. The life God gives us and renews in us comes in the social and historical forms common to any age and place. God came to Israel as a Jew, born to a woman pregnant outside of marriage and to an ordinary believer, about whom people snickered, "Why, isn't this **Joseph's** son!!?" Only to those with eyes to see and ears to hear was God's redemption and salvation present in Jesus' finite, fragile human life.

Eyes to see and ears to hear God's scandalous redemption at work among us is what we seek to form, nurture, and support in one another. Adults will resist conforming to the youth culture; youth will return the favor resisting conformity to the adult culture: both are right. For Christians seek mutual conformation to no specific **culture**. As members of Christ's risen and living body, Christians conform ourselves to God's Holy Spirit that indwells and is incarnate in every human situation and culture.

<u>Formation includes critique, for mature commitment calls for the ability to discern and to make judgments</u>. Part of the church's ministry is to form one another mutually. This calls us to allow ourselves to be known both by confessing the center of our faith and by clearly identifying the limits of what we believe is acceptable. Heated disagreement does not hinder bonded compassion, but personal judgment distances and alienates us from one another. Conversations that include critique of the church and its leaders are appropriate when we are also self-critical, letting our bonded compassion be as clear as our questions or dissent. For we seek to grow in and as Christ's body, the church, knowing that God loves us and offers us the generosity of heart and compassion to love, all

of our sisters and brothers--including those from whose actions we dissent and those whom we dislike as people.

"Formation" remains a difficult concept for us, in part because it asks each of **us** to leave what we know and to move into what is new to us. This makes us uneasy because we are uncertain, and we desire to be confidently certain. Yet, where we are in the life-long process of formation, our spiritual center is alive because of the new things God is doing among us.

o What does "formation" mean to you?

o What does your congregation do that helps infants, children, youth, young adults, and adults grow and practice, nurture and internalize, and embody and mature in their identity as Christians in the Church of the Brethren? What liturgical practices, celebrations, dramas, projects, teachings, foster Christian identity at each stage in the lives of individual members and the corporate church "person?" What understanding of God, church, and ministry will children and youth absorb from their experiences of the church's life and practices?

o Drawing on your own positive and negative experiences, what "steps" in the formation of a person's identity as a Christian and members of the Church of the Brethren can you identify in your congregation's life and practice which nurture and support our ministry and desire to grow at each point in a person's life? How can each of these "formation" experiences be made stronger and more positive for the congregation and its members?

Training and Support

<u>A number of crucial issues cluster around training and support for ministry</u>. What sort of training structures are appropriate for which contexts as we seek quality ministry? What sort of financial and other support structures are necessary for candidates for the ordained ministry to attain training for quality ministry, and then remain in ministry?

The congregation's crucial role as a partner in the training and support for set-apart ministries became increasingly clear to us.

The quality of training and support we expect for the ministry of all members effects how we think of and provide for the church's ordained ministers. Like calling and formation, training and support call for personal engagement. Important as programs and curricula are, it is more important that we are connected to each person and support them as they grow in their ability to minister. When we view training and support for ministry fundamentally as establishing and carrying out quality programs to "produce" good ministers, it is easy to objectify and distance ourselves from people, seeming to hold control over their lives. Growth in mutual ministry is not compatible with a spirit that manages people in order to solve their problems or to transform them. Congregations and persons whose formation has led them to respond to the call to ministry know their need for training and support. Building on their own experience, they support others with engaged honesty, integrity, courage, and compassion, offering to those they mentor what they have learned is essential for their spiritual growth and discipline.

Training and support always requires us to speak the truth in love. We are tempted to be nice, to say only what supports the other person, and to avoid the hard questions or comments. Such a response supports people at the cost of preparing them for ministry. It teaches them to seek approval rather than to perceive reality clearly and choose to grow. Our desire for others to be accountable takes shape as we speak and act with honesty, integrity, courage and compassion. Speaking the truth in love upbuilds us by opening our understanding to another's understanding. Support that speaks and receives the truth in love is basic to the ministry training essential for a community of compassionate ministers.

Congregations are partners in theological education. In our changing society, seminary education is increasingly capital-intensive. All partners in ministry in the Church of the Brethren-congregations, districts, the General Board, and the seminary--must seek ways to decapitalize and decentralize ministry training in our changing context. This would enable us to train and support more people for ministry, and would make seminary education attainable for those unable to afford the current costs. The cost of quality theological education is a major factor in training those preparing to enter the salaried ministry. Tuition at Bethany Theological Seminary presently pays about 14% of what it costs to educate students. Even so, the debts students incur relative to the salaries they can expect to receive make it unlikely that some students can earn enough in the salaried ministry to repay their debts.

Many congregations and districts help their own students financially. We hope that all Church of the Brethren congregations will financially support persons who are training for the ordained ministry, whether or not "their" students are in seminary. Local churches could "adopt" students in seminary, supporting them in fellowship and prayer as well as financially, and so help them to prepare for service to the whole church. Such support is much like the earlier style of Brethren mission involvement, an involvement that had strong local along with denominational ties. Similarly, this connection to local congregations could translate the strengths of the traditional unsalaried ministry and of Anthony Bloom ways of **forming and calling** people in ministry for ministry training and support. Active partnership between seminary and congregation is particularly vital when students come to seminary with a young, inexperienced or untested faith.[8]

When students receive congregational support during and for their training, their sense of having been called to serve the church is strengthened. When ministers in training feel they are "on their own" financially and spiritually, the salaried ministry begins to resemble any other job for which one trains and from which one hopes to make a living. Salary is, however, an important value for most members of the Church of the Brethren today. On the whole, we, like other middle-class Americans, relate status and salary. This means that what we pay pastors influences our esteem for them. Knowing the difference among congregations in their ability to pay pastors, the Annual Conference committee on pastoral compensation has sometimes designated salary increases by dollar amount rather than by percentage. This means more highly paid ministers are not as easily priced out of the market and starting pastors may catch up faster. Even so, local churches need to ask how we who affirm the "priesthood of all believers" view and value our salary, both in relation to the salary of one pastor and in relation to the salaries of others in the church family.

Support is as essential as training if the women and men we would like to have as set-apart ministers are to sense the church's call accompanying them as they move into a vocation with a salary scale well below what their abilities and education would command in other fields for which they are qualified. An important indicator of how we view the pastoral ministry and salary is whether we have urged our children to consider entering the church's salaried ministry and leadership.

At this time, when seminary education is extremely costly both for the church and for persons training for the salaried ministry, we find the model of minister of training exemplified in Education for a Shared Ministry and the model of unsalaried, "free" or bivocational ministry attractive for economic reasons. Perhaps the economy is a way God lures us to think creatively about ministry training and the practice of ministry as a church. On the other hand, both Education for a Shared Ministry and the unsalaried ministry require the geographical stability of church members in order to flourish. And geographical stability is increasingly rare among us.

Different forms of and places for ministry call for corresponding support and training structures. Wherever possible, a support partnership between the districts, the General Board, the seminary, congregations, and other persons in ministry is desirable. Ministry is well supported when the support systems are multiple and mutually accountable, and when the focus of both seminary education and other ministry training engages the minister, the congregation, and their growth together in ministry.

Recognizing the advantages and limits of Church of the Brethren ministry polity and policy is a crucial matter for the church's leaders. Identifying and serving within our proper limits is important for healthy congregational and district life. Congregations need to view themselves as serving the ministry of the whole church; districts need to refrain from intruding into or taking over local church life and decision making.

Lack of consistency among districts with regard to policy and polity makes receiving and transferring ordained ministers on behalf of the whole church more difficult. On the one hand, more consistent polity is desirable. On the other hand, we know that polity guidelines in themselves are inadequate for discerning what spirit is actually served. We do not want clear polity to lure us into serving the letter of polity rather than God's Spirit when we make administrative decisions.

Pastoral ministers continue to need support, yet especially those in the salaried ministry seem particularly to lack adequate support. District executives often feel they are the only ones supporting salaried pastors, particularly the young, first-time, and recently transferred pastors. By contrast, in Education for a Shared Ministry and the unsalaried ministry the built-in mentoring for training often continues as a support system in ministry. This difference in healthy support systems for ministers is related to the difference between the models of ministry. The unsalaried ministry and Education for a Shared Ministry assume an understanding of ministry in which the skills and gifts of all members are essential for church to be church. Where salaried ministers are employed, both they and the congregation often view the pastor as the one who "does" ministry for the whole church. Congregations and ministers alike find that a genuinely **professional**[9] minister, salaried or not, helps lead the whole church in the ministry to which all are called and sealed in baptism.

Pastors also need support because, although trained to respond to others' needs, they often fear making their own needs visible, lest they be seen as too weak to lead. It is important for pastors to embody for others that we can confess our needs and still live from our faith. Indeed, pastors' unclarity about their needs leads to confusion between their needs and those of others, often with the result that they seek to meet their needs by "helping" others. Like people who love, live with, and protect substance abusers, pastors can get addicted to helping others.

People whose lives are spent taking care of people who refuse to take care of themselves are called co- or counter-dependents because their lives are organized around others' needs and dependencies.[10] The inability to be clear about one's own needs corresponds with the inability to distinguish between reinforcing another's abusive addictions and supporting another's genuine growth. It is easy to confuse ministry with making people feel good and it is dangerous to think of ministry as meeting others' needs, especially when people in ministry are not clear about their own dependencies and needs. Hidden needs in all of us puts us in danger of becoming addicted to helping dependency addicts, of becoming voluntary victims rather than ministers. The tendency to control others by managing their situations or to care for others by meeting their needs indicates the spiritual immaturity of a person who does not yet recognize their need to be needed. The tendency to practice ministry by taking care of others or by making them feel good is more common among persons with little congregational mentoring who self-select for the set-apart ministry than among those whose life and work in a congregation has resulted in their being called to the set-apart ministry.

Healthy ministers, unsalaried or salaried, lay or ordained, can clarify their needs without organizing other's energy around their needs. Healthy ministers are also able to distinguish between addictive behavior patterns and temporary crisis responses, and able to discern when to hold others accountable for their behavior without anger or abandonment and when to stand with others in support. Adequate training and support of ministers--salaried and unsalaried pastoral ministers and ministers in the marketplace or neighborhood--is reflected not only in their skills and knowledge, but also in the attitude and spirit with which they give and receive support within the communion of saints.

The matter of financial support for pastors is difficult. Pastors' education, skills, and salary are very diverse. Even those with the same seminary education are not all paid on scale. Yet both pastors and churches work to continue education and pastoral growth, and to support adequately if minimally, pastors when the "norm" we like to assume is absent. Churches and pastors alike, however, relate salary to respect. Churches, like church members, pay for what we want. It is not acceptable to expect pastors to live by the "cross" as a servant when most congregational members live by the achievement-seeking "ladder."[11] Churches able to address the matter of pastoral salary support seriously may be able to address the economics of all its members and their ministries.

We asked what it might mean to have standard pastoral salaries. We wondered whether the whole church would be better served if a congregation's ability to pay scale were not a consideration in answering the call to ministry. We thought not, fearing that standardized pastoral salaries would disconnect the direct, practical relation between a local church's economic life and its ministerial accountability.

These conversations made us aware anew just how difficult it is for sisters and brothers in the church "family" to speak plainly about economic resources. While other topics may elicit more passion, none seems so taboo in the sense that we avoid considering its implications for our faith and for our practice as ministers, as disciples, as members of Jesus Christ. The Ananias and Sapphira story is powerful in this context because, like we, they wanted both to conceal their economic reality and to be held in high esteem for their exemplary economic behavior.

In the course of our conversation, our attention was called to contemporary consultations of representatives of the first and radical reformation churches in which all were challenged to commit ourselves to an economic ratio of no greater than 1:3 within our church institutions. Any size and scope of group might covenant to live this way: a group of friends or colleagues, a Sunday School class, a church executive committee or witness commission, one or several congregations, a district or church institution, a denomination. Initial questions the group would need to answer, of course, are whether to establish the 1:3 ratio based on income before or after taxes? How to relate salaried to wage-and-hour people? How to consider various sorts of benefits? When these questions are clear and practice begins, a whole new set of questions emerges: what do we do with the economic difference generated? When are children part of the decision-making process? In what way is "our" child's inheritance or our retirement put at risk because of our commitment to a larger economic family unit?

<u>While much has changed about the training and support needs for ministry over the years, all quality ministry calls for a deep personal spirituality, a love of people, as well as specific skills</u>. The "feminization of ministry"[12] has re-awakened the church's awareness that spirituality and a love for others are necessary "soil" in which to plant ministry skills. Recalling the unsalaried, Anthony Bloom, and Education for a Shared Ministry models of ministry, we recognize that an elaborate knowledge of data, while crucial to academic ministry training, is not always essential for persons to become excellent pastoral ministers. Indeed, our society has become so drenched in data and content that both are deemphasized at the popular level.[13] By contrast, multicultural literacy material[14] is increasingly important for providing communication and relationships in a world where the walls that formerly separated us are crumbling about our feet: walls we desire, and walls that offend us; walls by which we have distinguished between cultures, religions, economies, nations, classes, races, ages, sexes.

o What support would you like for your ministry? What forms of support do you give others in the ministry of all in the church?

o What support does your church give people you call into the set-apart ministry? What support does your church and do you provide for youth entering vocational and professional training?

o For what reasons do you think we should or should not expect and call for different kinds and amounts of support (money, letters, reports, etc.) for people who are training for salaried ministry and/or for the ministry of all in their vocations, neighborhoods, and homes?

Quality

Quality has been addressed in at least four ways in our conversations: first, by identifying three aspects of quality essential to ministry, namely: spirituality, love of people, and specific skills such as preaching and counseling; second, by refusing identification of criteria and characteristics that convey quality in candidates; third, by resisting gatekeeping measures relative to ministerial candidates and; fourth, by confessing that we hesitate to call out those whom we see to be most gifted.

Brethren usually refuse studies done with an eye to reliably identifying who is likely to "make it" in ministry, even when such tests are not based on academic achievement or ability. Our reasons for not using such tests to discern possible difficulties or to guide those who come to us for counsel vary. We have seen that some people who test one way work out another way in practice. We know that congregational needs are as varied as are the persons who prepare for the set-apart ministry. We are aware that serious handicaps may, when acknowledged and attended to, become resources for ministry. One district executive simply stated the refusal to reliance on tests: "It makes me feel dirty."

Although we doubt reliance on tests, we also question our doubt. We have seen how hard it is for Brethren to say "no" to anyone who feels anything strongly. We fear that limit-setting will be interpreted as a betrayal of a sister or brother. Wanting to be liked and disliking to speak the truth in love when the words are hard, Brethren often encourage people in directions where they are unlikely to experience a fit in ministry.

The Brethren tendency to encourage people who show few signs of readiness for ministry is related to our formation as a church. We see that Roman Catholics place emphasis on Christian formation.[15] In contrast, we, along with other reformation, radical reformation, and free churches, emphasize transformation. Churches who view formation as fundamental place enormous energy on how persons, families, and churches are first shaped. The fundamental concern is to nurture a quality of spirit and attitude that is recognizably Christian: a quality able to re-adapt itself to or endure social and cultural change. In contrast, our Church of the Brethren emphasis on transformation assumes that people can and do change, that people can and do overcome what is absent from or negative in early experiences. Both emphases are accurate. Both are important for our understanding of training for quality ministry.[16]

When Brethren overlook the significance of formation, we forget that we can train only what is there. Indeed, our emphasis on transformation, which releases gifts and develops abilities, presupposes formation. One way we understand the urgent call for more spiritual depth and direction today is to recognize that in the effort to acquire skills and data we have too often disregarded our spiritual attitudes, leaving our hearts undernourished.

Perhaps tests can be developed to help us identify where candidates for ministry training are well formed and where they need further training or transformation. Such assessment would allow the training of persons with a strong faith formation and experience in congregational life to concentrate on honing skills and providing data, a task for which seminaries are well-suited. By the same measure, persons still in need of faith formation, tested

Christian identity, or experience in congregational life, might begin as ministry interns, as mentees in a congregation whose life and ministry will surround and support as well as guide them.

The status of ordained, salaried ministers continues to decline in contemporary North American Anglo culture. The Church of the Brethren may feel this change less than other communions, perhaps because our traditions of ministry have included the call of all church members and because our tradition of calling set-apart leaders has included calling persons into unsalaried ministries. In most stable communities where our churches are strong, unsalaried ordained ministers **are also** professionals: farmers, business people, managers, bankers, shopkeepers, skilled tradeswomen and men, etc.

Though ministry has suffered a status loss, the role and leadership expectations placed upon set-apart ministers is no less demanding.[17] As recently as prior to World War II, to be a minister meant assurance of the community's respect and appreciation. Now to be a minister by profession is more likely to result in low esteem from the surrounding community. Both who is attracted and who we call into the church's ordained ministry have changed. We have responded to the cultural devaluation of ministerial status, as is indicated by the fact that parents and respected adults in the community rarely challenge our most able youth, young adults, and second career folks to consider a call to the church's ordained ministry.

Unsalaried and salaried ministries are concerned for quality in the sense that throughout their ministry they feel "I'd better be prepared". Moreover, in past generations, "free" ministers were very often the church's most qualified professionals. They had studied scripture, read theology, traveled widely to confer with other leaders, and were involved in community affairs as well as with members and leaders of other churches and other faith traditions. What has changed today is that unsalaried ministers are often the least professionally trained among the church's ordained clergy and that the very word "professional" has become problematic. Indeed, one reason we speak of "unsalaried" rather than "free" ministers is to counter the cultural implication that free means unprofessional. At the same time, however, when the church's basic concern for its ordained leaders is that they excel and exhibit management know-how, fundraising, public relations techniques, and organizational strategies, professionalism has already moved to the center of the church's faith and practice.

The notions of "quality" and "professional" have had an odd relationship among Brethren. For the generation now moving toward retirement, ministry as "profession" meant having standards and expectations for ministry. Professional meant preparing for ministry in orderly, supervised ways that provided clear measures to help the minister know when he or she was growing in ways that would strengthen their ministry. In such a context, "quality" ministry and "professional" ministry seemed very close together. But, from another perspective and given other presuppositions, Leonard Sweet's critique that contrasts ladder and cross, profession and calling, also makes sense. There is no simple "answer" to the question about ministry as profession, especially for a people prone to excuse poor quality because "people are called."

We asked ourselves whether our preoccupation with financial security adds to our ambiguity about ministry. We suspect that one reason we are lured from the church's set-apart and "universal" ministries is that we churchwomen and men have a split identity. In day-to-day practice, we respond to much the same values as those with whom we live and work. This often means that we confess and teach values we forget and deny in our daily actions.

o What value do you place on the set-apart ministry as a vocation?

o Have you called persons of quality into set-apart ministry? How do you identify "quality" or "quality ministry leadership?" Do you <u>want</u> persons of quality as your set-apart leaders?

o Does "quality leadership" mean the same thing in all congregations, settings, situations?

o How do you respond to people who feel called or want to be pastors, but in whom you fail to see the basic qualities for ministry, and whom you would not want as your pastor?

o What aspects of "quality" are particularly important for persons entering the set-apart ministry?

o What quality expectations do you have for the ministry of all members? Talk about how "quality" similarities and differences relate to different sorts of ministry tasks, different people, different situations. What quality expectations do you have for the **relations** among all members as ministers?

Spirituality

> **These conversations led us to believe that our spirituality is deeply connected with our leadership crisis. As we consider our own commitments and values, we confess our ambivalence about ministry: an ambivalence that often sends double signals to those about us. We wrestled with how we as churchwomen and men may be at once too influenced by our culture, and also out of touch with some very significant social forces moving around us.**

It is difficult to identify the source of our ambiguity about ministry, especially since all of us in these conversations want to be and, in various ways, are in ministry. Some of us are in the ministry of all and some in the church's "professional" and/or set-apart ministries. Although ministry is our life, we also know we communicate ambiguity. We seek to identify its source. We know this is a question of how our faith effects our life. It is a spiritual concern that will not be changed by the establishment of excellent programs. Others have no power to heal us or transform from our ambiguity. Neither can we "make" a change by force of our own will. We believe that, while we are unable to make this change by the strength of our choice, it also will not occur apart from both our choice and our intentional exercise of appropriate spiritual disciplines.

We began by noting that our relationship to society and culture is unhealthy. In one way, we feel and are disconnected from our culture. In another and more traditional way, we are grounded in the we-they thinking that shows up in our conversation and action. For example, when we disagree with and dislike the values, practices, and realities of other people and groups, we wonder why "others" do not change things. We create inner distance from what we dislike, yet we offer "solutions" to and call for change in people whose lives we do not engage.

However disconnected we feel or want to be from our culture, we are also deeply influenced by the society in which we live. Our complicity in reinforcing contemporary cultural values by practicing them ourselves is vast. For example, we are largely a white, suburban, middle-class people who, judging by the shape and color of our local churches, want to stay this way. We seek church growth and ecological, economic, military and global responsibility, but we keep personal distance as we write position papers, contribute cash, volunteer time, and return home to an unchanged life. We scramble for success as we run our farms, businesses, and church institutions by the "the bottom line". The required financial disclosure of our income and possessions when we seek student aid for our youth to attend college is perhaps the most privately sheltered information in our lives.

Roof and McKinny, in American Mainline Religion, claim that churches rarely "lose" members to other churches. It is true that persons "born" Brethren do join Methodist, Unitarian, Presbyterian, Episcopal, and other churches, often when they move and find no healthy churches of their formative community present. But most churches gain about as many as they lose in this process. Roof and McKinny claim that many persons brought up in the church simply leave the church altogether and enter the secular society. This study reinforced our conviction that spirituality is directly related to the quality of the church's ministries: the ministry of all; set-apart ministries; and the ordained ministry.

We are puzzled and concerned that sisters and brothers debunk one another or particular groups of Christians, e.g. charismatic Christians. In one way, charismatic leadership has always been important to the Church of the Brethren. The authority of our pastors "has" to be largely charismatic, since the congregation is the pastor's boss.[18] Yet in the 20th century, we have too often seen charismatic leadership become demonic: Adolf Hitler is only the most obvious example. We are equally concerned when some members uncritically wrap their arms about and identify with groups they do not intimately know. Both the self-defensively critical and the flounderingly uncritical responses to persons who offer leadership in the church make it difficult to train and live as set-apart ministers in and for the church.

Quality leaders are also always people whose lives and words are one. It is not enough for our words to say what is right and good, but to have mastered rhetoric to convince peoples' minds. Unless in our hearts we "believe enough in what we say to invite others to join us" in living our commitment, our rhetoric about Jesus as our way, truth, and life will be empty and lifeless.

Congregations in ministry are communities that mentor all who worship there in and for ministry. Active concern for the ministry of all may "name the gifts" of each, helping everyone identify their talents for service so all who are part of the church as covenanted community grow in their commitment and ability to minister in the church and in their daily life of in homes, neighborhoods, and jobs. When a congregation identifies and nurtures each person's gifts for ministry, it is more than a "partner" in ministry training. It is the foundation on which the denominational ministry training is built. For as each local church calls, forms, trains and supports each and everyone mutually in and for ministry, quality ministry is manifest as the external shape of the inner spiritual life of a people whose life as church is ministry.

o What do you understand by "spirituality?"

o What do you think of when you hear the words, "spiritual crisis"? How do you know who and whose you are? What tensions and conflicts do you find in your life? Why are you church members? Why do you follow Christ? serve God? seek to be good people? care about your friends? care about gaining community prestige? desire to be accepted as trustworthy?

o What moves and motivates you most in making vocational choices? in doing volunteer work? in deciding how to use your money? How and when are you influenced by this culture, though you may not realize or resist it until later, for example, what do you own that you do not need?

o How does the way you live "tell" children in the church what it means to be a Christian in the Church of the Brethren?

CHAPTER TWO

A PROPHETIC SPIRITUALITY: PEOPLE IN MINISTRY

Rosemary Haughton

PROPHETIC PEOPLE
(Jeremiah 8: 17-22, 9: 17-24)

As we come together at a time like this, as people of faith seeking a way forward, we have to consider first of all where we stand in our time in history. We stand in a time of unprecedented hope in many ways, a time in which people all over the earth--in Europe, in South Africa and in many other places--are rising up to claim their freedom and their future. It is a time of tremendous turmoil, of political change and challenge. We ask ourselves, is there finally the possibility of peace? And then we wonder what kind of peace? Will it be real peace or will it be, as Jeremiah says, "a cry of peace where there is no peace."

We also stand together in a time of unprecedented danger. Beyond the still existing misery and fear and oppression is the danger of environmental change that may bring to many millions greater poverty, greater threat of death. The readings from Jeremiah call up in us the feelings of a people confronted with sin and evil in the world. We wonder what to do, how to respond. What kind of people can minister in such a world? From what kind of people may the right kind of message, may God's message, be given?

In the book of Wisdom, we are reminded that "Wisdom enters into holy souls in every age and makes them friends of God and prophets." At this time, it is from prophetic people, from the prophetic community, that ministry might come to a world such as ours. A prophetic people. What does this mean? What do prophets do? What are prophets for?

Prophets are first of all people who are attuned to God, who have a perception of the presence and action of God in their lives as well as in the world around them, and who, therefore, have an attitude to the events of their time that springs from a perception of God in all events. Their perception of events springs from deep atunement to God. All that they do is based in a deeply attentive listening to God's reality in the world, in scripture, and in the history of people so that they are in touch with God, in touch with what God brings about.

What we are talking about is an attitude to life that belongs to the people who are called together by God. It is an attitude of listening to God's message, knowing that listening may lead to great challenges and may bring in new possibilities. In the first part of the reading from Jeremiah we just heard, the prophet was mourning for the evil he saw around him, for the desolation, for the loss. He was mourning for the hurt to people, but also for the hurt to the land. The fabric of a society was falling apart. We can think of this not only in terms of people whose homes were literally devastated, but also in terms of the people whose lives had been torn apart by the fear and uncertainty, by not knowing how they were going to manage. We can think of this in terms of people who had lost their homes and their land. Jeremiah wept at what he saw. He longed for peace and healing and cried out, "Where is the physician, has God forsaken us? What do we need? What is lacking that healing might come?"

But Jeremiah recognized that something more was needed before healing could begin. This, paradoxically, was more grieving. It seems as if the prophet at this point recognized that we can grieve in a superficial way and then, having cried out to God, assume that our God will move in and heal us. Jeremiah seems to have been reflecting on the fact that perhaps we have not allowed ourselves truly to grieve. We have not truly been in touch with what is wrong, with the roots of evil around us.

Jeremiah has a rather strange remedy for this lack of being in touch. He says we need the experts. We need people to teach us how to grieve. Traditionally, in most cultures, the women have been those in charge of the task of grieving. Even in cultures where they do not do it professionally, societies tend to expect grieving to be done by women. I think this is natural since women are the ones who are expected to allow themselves to feel and to express their feelings.

The prophet was saying that there is something in human beings that is represented by these mourning women, something we need to call up in order to liberate in all of us the power to grieve. It has to be done; we need to learn the task of grieving. Jeremiah makes it quite clear that grieving is a skill. Evidently in his mind this was not only something we need to learn, but something we need to teach each other so that we may allow ourselves to feel what is happening and respond to it, so that we may share with each other what we perceive and how we feel about it. It is a skill we have to learn and we have to teach each other. Jeremiah said, tell them to teach their daughters, tell them to teach their neighbors. So, in his mind, grieving is not something we can do once and for all. It is an ongoing task of a prophetic people. From generation to generation, we have to learn and relearn. We do not want to, and yet it is only if we are in touch with God's wisdom through grieving that justice and right begins to be possible. This is the work of a prophetic people. Jeremiah wants grieving and mourning to be learned and shared, so that the people may be aware of the destruction that is happening and will happen. He says very clearly that nothing else will do. Wisdom and riches and power are no substitute for this willingness to allow ourselves to feel and to share our feelings.

It is very difficult to allow ourselves to feel in this way. To some extent, we are right to not to allow ourselves to feel too much because there is only so much we can take. This is why grieving is the work of a community, the prophetic community. We cannot lay grieving on individuals because it is too hard. What happens when we lay grieving on individuals and refuse to allow it to be a public thing is that people turn to tranquilizers, drugs, entertainment, or to some other form of addictive denial, because it is too hard, because the individual cannot carry the grief. Grief needs compassion to be bearable: "compassion" means suffering together. We reflect upon what we read in the newspaper and see on television. We reflect upon the scripture that enables us to deal with what we read and see. We reflect upon the action that is called for. We do it together.

In the gospels we find Jesus doing the same thing. He grieves over the city, rages at what was done to the people, calls others to grieve, so that out of shared grief, anger and compassion change may begin. It is much easier to deny and we have so many mechanisms of denial. Some of these are necessary for our survival. We cannot live with a tremendous emotional burden day after day. Our tendency is to numb ourselves since we cannot face it.

To help each other, we have to begin, very simply, in our sharing of prayer and scripture. We have to gather in small groups and, in the context of prayer, talk about it how these things make us feel. We have to express our anger, our outrage. We have to allow each one to say whatever he or she feels like saying, even the exaggerated expressions or views. We have to try to experience the outrage that is God's outrage at what human beings have done to this earth and to God's people.

The task of healing will begin, in its own right time, because what happens when we allow ourselves this anger and grief, this prophetic raging, is that we become vulnerable. We are open; God can reach us. Yet it is a terrible experience, for we begin to understand how God feels. We begin to know from what depths of suffering and compassion justice and righteousness have to grow. Yet the sharing of grief is something that creates a community. When everybody at this conference here began to sing a capella, as people took up different parts and sang easily in harmony, I witnessed a real expression of the kind of thing that is at the heart of community. It is a marvelous symbol of what we are looking for. We are looking for a community that is able to undertake a prophetic vocation and so we are looking for a community that can be as much at one in feeling and thinking as voices are in raising that kind of song.

This community of music is immediate. It draws deeply from each person, and then from history. Every movement of change, every revolution, has had songs, has counted on this discovery of unity in music to bring people together, to put them in touch with each other. This is a very profound experience and a very profound symbol. And there is a kind of silent singing that we encounter when we are willing to share our feelings and our faith, our suffering and our hope. As a community of faithful people, we have to learn to listen to the women who have the skills we need. We heard a poem written by one such woman a little while ago: Julia Esquivel is a woman who understands grieving and who understands the joy that can come out of it.[1]

The first task of the prophet, then, is the tremendous task of grieving. This is the groundwork from which healing begins. The willingness to "suffer with" makes it possible to envisage ways to healing which are not arbitrary, which are not superficial, which can start at the point where suffering begins.

I sometimes have this kind of experience with the women who come to the shelter at Wellspring House in Gloucester, Massachusetts, the shelter where I work. These women, many of whom have been abused, express what women have learned for centuries to accept as a description of themselves. They view themselves as people who are <u>wrong</u>. They feel that what has been done to them is a punishment, that they deserve it. They may even joke about how life is for `bad' people like themselves. Then, when they come together in support groups, they begin to tell their stories. As they tell their stories, at first they tell them as statements about "how it is." But, after a while, they hear each other. They begin to realize their common experience; they begin to have compassion for each other. They begin to say, "It doesn't have to be like that. I am not an bad person. What has been done to me is not something I deserve." They begin to weep. They begin to rage. Out of this weeping and raging, they gradually gain a determination that says it will not be like it has been.

Of course, this does not happen all at once. There is always the possibility of sinking once more into the despair of the pain that so many people carry through their lives. But if there is a community, if there are others who can say "you are loved" and who can keep on saying it in words and in deeds, there is hope. All over the world, whole populations have suffered centuries of oppression. They have been taught that such oppression is what they are meant for, that it is what God wills and so they must bear it. The apathy grows, from generation to generation. What begins to break up this oppression is, first of all, grief and rage that can come through. People begin to be able to say to each other, "We didn't know . . . this is not God's will . . . God is not that kind of God." People begin to gather and to read scripture together, to form community, and to support each other in the search for the grief from which healing can begin.

This, then, is the first task of a prophetic people. It is the base from which everything else grows. It does not mean that we get over the grief and move to something more fun yet we must not get stuck in it. There is a kind of anger and grieving that puts up a wall against change. This is usually because anything new seems impossible. It is sometimes hard not to feel like this. We look at our nation, the wealthiest nation in the world, and yet we see a profound degree of despair and poverty among us. We look at the levels of oppression and misery in the Third World, at what is being done to people in El Salvador and in many other places, and it is hard not to despair. This why a prophetic people has to learn to grieve as a people of faith. A prophetic people has to learn to grieve with those who are despairing but not to despair about finding a way through. Healing and newness can begin because there is a physician, a physician known in the community. Therein we find God who is the healer and who give us the skills we need to heal each other and to reach out to a wounded world.

So the physician is within us. Work begins and newness begins with the strength of the community. We can begin to make decisions that compassion dictates, not rushing into anything that makes us feel better as compassionate people, but deeply understanding the roots of the evil. We, therefore, know whence comes the healing and what forms it may take in a practical way. This is why we need a prophetic people and why we need prophets. This is why we need people to whom ministry is the prophetic ministry of God's power. What are the kinds of ministry that can come out of this? A leadership of grieving, a leadership of hoping. We begin very simply by allowing each other to feel those things that God feels, to know the things that God knows about the world, about each other, about our neighbor, about our town, our city, our country, and then to grieve and to get in touch with the healing that is beginning.

DIVINE HOMEMAKING
(Jeremiah 31:1-9, 31-34)

Jeremiah, who spoke for the need for grieving, also spoke of the coming of change, the coming of hope, the coming of healing. He cried out and screamed and wept and called others to cry with him, for the people who have been in exile, the people who have been banished from the land that belonged to them, have come home. When the people are banished, when the people are in exile, God is in exile. This is not because God does not dwell in everyplace, but because human beings need to have a place where they can know God, a place that is their special place. The people's homecoming is also God's homecoming.

When the people came out of Egypt, they said, "We need to go and worship in the desert, we can't worship here in Egypt." The Egyptians might well have said "Why not? it's a perfectly good place, we'll lend you a temple!" But the people could not worship because in that place they were enslaved; it was not their place. They needed to be free. Freedom is a sense of ownership, a sense of belonging, a sense of being at home. However it happens, freedom creates a situation in which also God can be at home, in which people can be open to God because they have self-respect. So there is a sense in which God can come home only at human invitation, and God's tender calling to the people is wanting a response: "Come with us, we want to go home."

The second task of the prophet is, therefore, to announce this vision of homecoming. God's people have been exiled and now it is time for them to come home, because when the people are not welcome, then God is unwelcome. In our own country and in so many places in the world, people are in fact, geographically, exiled from their homes. But there are also millions of people in our country who are exiled in the sense that they have no ownership, no security, no sense that this is their place. They are pushed around. They are utterly dependent on other people. These are people who are homeless, who are jobless, or who have jobs but wonder whether they will make it or lose their jobs next week. These are people who live on the edge of homelessness, going from paycheck to paycheck, farmers who have lost their land, women who are economincally dependent on men. There are whole nations in many parts of the world which are dependent upon other nations for their existence: there is no home for these people. The earth is not home for so many millions, for so many who are dispossessed and alienated.

The task of prophetic community is thus extended to envisioning a new possibility, to envisioning how this homeless situation might change. It is extended to beginning to make change a concrete reality. There is one family I have come to know very well, a family from Texas. The husband worked in a high tech industry. The wife also worked with computers part-time and was brilliant at it. They had a good life and a large home with two cars. They volunteered in a local shelter and soup kitchen. They gave money; they took children in. They did all the things that people do when they have good will and are loving people with the faith and money with which to do good. Then the firm that employed the husband closed. He looked for jobs for weeks on end. He was told, "You won't get anything since all the other firms are closing too; you'll have to leave." It seemed to them their only hope was to go to the east where they had relatives. They sold their home for so little that they had just enough money to pay their debts. All they had left was a car--a not-very-good car for they sold their good one --with which to travel east. When they arrived their car broke down. They went to a welfare office, but were told, "You have no residence here, we can't help you." Somebody said, "Call Wellspring." We lent them a little money to stay in a motel and they went out looking for jobs: any jobs. The husband got a job as a waiter. For weeks, for months, they scraped by. They had four children, three of whom were in high school. The children went to school and worked in their spare time to try to keep things going. They lived in a winter rental motel. They paid the money they had borrowed from Wellspring back $5.00 a week and little by little things did get better. The husband was still not able to get the kind of job for which he was qualified, because nobody in industries wanted highly qualified people. He finally got a job in a camera store.

What this family lost, in addition to their home and their cars and their money, was their self-respect. They hung onto it; they tried to hang onto it. But even now, two years later, when they have recovered to some extent through their tremendous hard work, where they have managed to find an apartment they can afford, and when both are working, although not very well paid, they find it hard to believe that anyone can respect them. They know what the welfare system is like from the inside. They know the kind of abuse that welfare officers feel themselves entitled to pour out on people who come to them, although this is the help those who ask for it have paid for as taxpayers. They know what it is like not to be able to pay the bills, not to have enough money to get decent food for the children. They know what it is like to borrow and shuffle and live from day-to-day. The thing that happened to these people was not just poverty; it was the experience of dependence and alienation. Nobody wanted to know them, or at least they felt that nobody did. They were ashamed. They were the dispossessed: dispossessed by what seemed a fluke. A few years before they had been among, if not the wealthy, the comfortable and, it seemed, the secure.

My friendship with these people taught me a lot about what can happen to people emotionally when they are treated with no respect because they have no money, because they have no work. There are so many people in our society who have lived through similar experiences, not just for a few months, but all of their lives. It becomes a way of living. They know they have no security. They know they do not count. They do not vote. Why should they? These, then, are the people who are exiles. These are the people whom God wants to call home. These are the people whom it is the church's work as a prophetic community to call home.

How are we to become a community who can do this? In the second part of the reading of Jeremiah, we heard the famous passage in which God says that the knowledge of God, the knowledge of

God's love, will be placed in people's hearts and they will not even need to teach others. Something happens to people in certain circumstances that enables them to be in touch with God. Something enables them to be in touch with what God wants, with God's law in this sense, with how God sees things and want things to be. This passage says they do not need to teach each other. Does that mean we do not tell each other what we understand, that we have nothing to share with each other, that we cannot teach? I do not think it means any of these things. I think this passage means that what is not appropriate is some people's claim to expert knowledge with the implication that other people are entirely ignorant and have nothing to contribute. This is the kind of attitude many people have towards those who are not regarded as full citizens, toward the ones who do not belong. But the knowledge of God in people's hearts is something that, on the contrary, we need to elicit from each other. The message is that we may help people claim this way of listening to what happens, listening to scripture and listening to world events. This listening will help us to realize how God is moving in events and where God is calling.

Working with homeless women I have, together with other people, shared the experience of realizing how hard it is to believe that people who are deprived, who have lived a life of abuse and rejection, and who have very little self confidence, really do have in themselves the knowledge that is the knowledge of God. This knowledge is promised to all people created in God's image and yet they themselves do not know they have it. It is first of all the task of the prophetic community in this context to believe--really believe--that there is in <u>all</u> people the knowledge of God which we have learned to share with each other, (knowledge of God we who are so privileged receive daily, weekly), and to believe people can be helped to discover it. We do not have to tell them, as it said in the passage from Jeremiah. What we have to do is help people discover that they <u>know</u> it, help them discover what they know, believe what they know, trust it, move on it.

I think that this is the way in which the prophetic people leads the homecoming. The prophetic people leads the coming home of the least and the weakest, as Jeremiah describes it: the coming home of the ones who, in a sense, can barely walk and yet of whom God says "their way will be made smooth." They will have what they need, they will be lovingly cared for. This caring comes from those who are called to lead the way home. The prophet's vision of the homecoming is very practical. People are to plant vineyards, replacing the vineyards that were devastated and the farms that were destroyed when the people of Israel, as Jeremiah had foreseen, went into exile. When the people come back, as Jeremiah had also foreseen, they were to rebuild, to replant, to recreate what was laid waste. It was at this point, then, that they would be able to celebrate: experience the joy of coming home.

Some months ago in the Christian Science Monitor, an article described how people across this country are discovering that, in town planning, we do not have to keep residence and business and farming in separate compartments. People are discovering it is more human, more acceptable, and much more fun, to have multiple zoning, so people can live over the stores, walk to work, walk to the cinema, and walk to school. Some years ago, a book was written by a Christian minister in England about the same thing: a vision for the next century that included the recovery of the village-type of community. I mention these things here because they echo Jeremiah's very practical sense about what people do when they come home to create community, to create a situation in which people can build their houses, plant their gardens, and then celebrate because they belong. God's law, written in people's hearts, helps them to understand what they need to become neighbors and friends. This is the extraordinary vision the prophet puts before us: a vision of people coming into their own homes, being able to claim them, because God's law is written in their hearts.

There is a story by Hans Anderson that many of you may have read when you were young, or perhaps you read it to your children. It is called The Snow Queen. It is the story of a little boy and girl who were great friends. Through the breaking of an evil mirror that distorts all goodness reflected in it, a splinter of glass gets lodged in the boy's heart, and he loses touch with the warmth and goodness of home. Every good thing looks alien and evil to him. He becomes cold, distant, and alienated, and wanders off into the cold regions of the Snow Queen. Gerda, his little friend, travels far and wide looking for him because she loves him. She is rather like God as described in the passage from Jeremiah, looking for the people in the wilderness, wanting to bring them home. Gerda, the prophet, is looking for the lost. When she finally finds him, he does not want her. He does not want human feelings. He does not belong. But when Gerda weeps, the warmth of her tears touches the ice around his heart and melts it. He begins to feel her grief, he weeps and the splinter of glass is washed from his eye. Then he begins to discover again the capacity for joy. He begins to go home. When Kay and Gerda come out of the cave of ice, the ice disappears and flowers begin to grow. They walk home through the spring that is blossoming around them. When the numbness is melted, when people grieve together, they can also rejoice together. They can begin to rebuild.

There is a passage from Isaiah 55 about the possibility of rebuilding in people's hearts of their knowledge of what they can be to each other: the recreation of a genuine community. "Break out into shouts of joy," the prophet said, "lead the nations." This is surely the task of the church: to lead the nations into joy by being people who are able to lead others home, having first come home ourselves. This prophetic ministry becomes possible when people help each other to melt the ice in their hearts, help each other to grieve, and then help each other to create newness in very practical ways.

Prophetic ministry, therefore, has to do with town planning, with the way we farm, with how we use the land. It has to do with how employment is set up, with giving people security and self-respect. Prophetic ministry has to do with how law and order is applied, and not just applied to the poor. It is very nitty-gritty stuff, this prophetic ministry. And, indeed, in many places in the prophetic books the prophetic ministry is spelled out. The prophetic community leads God's people home. It is a kind of divine homemaking.

At this time in the history of our planet, we know as we have never realized before just how easily we could lose this home, our only home. And yet God calls us to transform it. Jesus called us to recognize the coming of the reign of God and called people to make God's reign a reality. This can be done; it depends on us. We are called to be divine homemakers, and when we have created the home, we have a party. We come with "jingles," as it says in one translation, with "timbrels," according to another translation, with things that make a nice noise, a celebrative noise. And, again, it is the women who do the celebrating in scripture. Jeremiah, in particular, is very aware of the right brain quality of the prophetic vocation, of the feminine feeling in men and women that is needed to seize both grief and joy. It is prophetic awareness breaking out into celebration. God is saying to us, "This is how human life is meant to be. This is how human life can be, because I am a mother and father to my people. I make a home for them, and I need those who will call home the one's who have been driven away and lost." This is the work of God's wisdom that "in every age enters into holy souls and makes them friends of God, and prophets."

"FEAR NOT, LITTLE FLOCK"
(Luke 12:32-34)

I have two translations of the scripture passage, a passage which is very short. The first one we heard read is the Revised Standard Version.[2] The other, from the New English Bible, is a little bit different and is helpful in giving us a different feel of the passage.

> Have no fear, little flock, for your Father has chosen to give you the kingdom. Sell your possessions, and give in charity; provide for yourselves purses that do not wear out, and never failing treasure in heaven, where no thief can get near it, nor moth destroy it. For where your treasure is, there will your heart be also.

I think as we read any scriptures, we have to be aware of the background and ask who wrote it, for whom, and what were the preoccupations of the writer. I think this helps to remember Luke used the material available to him for the particular needs of the congregation he was addressing. In all of Luke's gospel and in the Acts of the Apostles, the author had a special concern for people who had money, people who were on the wealthy side, although not necessarily very rich, but who were doing pretty well and were concerned about their influence, about what was required of them as converts to the Way.

In this particular passage, we see a typical Lukan connection that tries to help people recognize they must "hang loose" from their possessions while they are awaiting the expected coming of Christ. We recognize that, in order to help people face those kind of decisions, Luke chose his material from a particular point of view. Our task is to try to understand perhaps the different perspective, in some cases the very different perspective, of the words of Jesus at the time they were spoken. Luke, like any person writing, chooses what suits his purpose and arranges the material in a way that makes a particular point, even though it may not be exactly the same point Jesus was making when he originally spoke those words. The kind of message in this passage is clearly one that was very important for Jesus' immediate followers. I think the emphasis has to do with a particular stage in the development of the little gathering, the "little flock" that was those followers of Jesus during his earthly lifetime.

These were people of many different kinds, men and women, for we are not just talking about the twelve, but about the quite large gathering of people who had attached themselves to Jesus. They had, in their early sense of the tremendous power of his calling, simply dropped whatever they were doing to follow. In those days of the early Galilean ministry, there was tremendous excitement. The crowds were growing greater and greater. The enthusiasm and hope, along with the sense of the possibility of liberation, were growing among the people. Wherever they went, the disciples of Jesus were followed by crowds of enthusiastic people expecting colossal changes immediately. I think perhaps what has been happening in Eastern Europe recently can give us a feeling of what this tremendous excitement was like. Suddenly there was the feeling that barriers had gone down and anything was possible. For a while, nothing else matters; the practical things are not even considered as we are just swept along in the excitement of it all.

These early followers of Jesus were people in love. Their new discovery, their new relationship with the Father, their new relationship with Jesus who had called them, had taken over their whole lives. Everything else was transformed within this experience. They had a tremendous vision of God's reign breaking in at any moment and were convinced nothing was ever going to be the same again. There was going to be everlasting peace and plenty. Of course, they were drawing on the scriptures they had all heard since childhood, scriptures of the prophecies of the reign of God that would transform the world. Particularly from Isaiah--we know how precious the book of Isaiah was to Jesus himself-- they had heard so often the great prophecies of a time of peace, a time of prosperity, a time when people would no longer destroy each other. They had heard of a time when there would be no longer any disease, when children would grow up in safety, when people would be, in the words of Isaiah, "able to build houses and live in them and grow gardens and eat their fruit." They had heard this message that said that no longer would people be exploited to provide homes or food for the owners of the land while they themselves lived in squalor and hunger.

The people had a whole sense of something tremendous changing in their lives. There would be no sickness and no disaster. Jesus would drive away all evil as he was quite visibly doing in the lives of the people around him. And yet the weeks went on and the months went on and other elements crept into the situation. There was a lot of hostility. Even these excited and expectant people, swept up in the euphoria of passionate love, began to recognize it was not going to be easy and not going to be quick. The people they had been taught from childhood to respect as their leaders and teachers, in many cases, became very suspect. And these leaders, in turn, were beginning to treat the disciples with suspicion. Some among the disciples' own friends and families were not at all happy with what they were doing. Alongside this, there must have been a growing awareness of the sheer quantity of pain and anger surrounding them. The pain and danger, indeed, were motivating people to come to Jesus. But the crowds of people were bringing with their sickness, their despair, their anger, also the possibility of disillusion.

When you live in your own place and you are getting along with your own life, when you are very busy, you know there is suffering, you know there are people who are very sick or who have been evicted because they could not pay their taxes. Perhaps you know in the back of your mind these things might happen to you. But, somehow, as long as your life keeps going, your focus is on making it manageable.

The disciples of Jesus were pulled out of relatively comfortable living and were suddenly confronted with crowds of people who were desperately hoping for a change. These crowds of people lived lives that were nearly intolerable, that were oppressed by taxes they could not pay and that were constantly threatened by the loss of everything. Many of these people were small farmers who had already lost everything. They were angry people as well as sick people. As months went by, this confrontation with the crowds must have been a very difficult experience for the men and women who had chosen to follow Jesus because they felt everything had suddenly changed.

But not all the evil had been overcome. Even Jesus could not heal everybody. There was no conquering progress; but there were people criticizing, blaming, denouncing, people they had learned all their lives to respect. So some of the disciples began to have second thoughts; they began to worry. What is going to happen when the money runs out? I need new shoes. What is going to happen to the roof of my house if it is not repaired before the rainy season comes? Who is going to look after my possessions while I am away? In other words, if the reign of God is not breaking in right here and now, life has to go on somehow. What are we going to do? Some left and went home. Some of them grumbled, as we know. Even the most faithful ones were troubled, wondering how it all fit, and were worried about the future.

I think it is out of this kind of experience that these Lukan sayings of Jesus come. Above all, like so many of his sayings, they are reassuring. "Do not be afraid." You do not tell people not to be afraid unless they are afraid. And Jesus addresses them as the "little flock," the word for God's chosen people in scripture. In so doing, he is reminding them they are the ones who have been chosen. They are the ones who have received the promise of the kingdom. They are the ones who are bound to inherit. "Fear not little flock" is both reassurance and promise.

They have been chosen by God; their very existence is part of the promise. This is very important. They are not being reassured individually. They are being reminded that, as the "little flock," the fact they exist as a community is part of the promise made by God. The Father has chosen them; it is the Father's pleasure to have them and choose them, to be among them, to call them out. It is the Father's pleasure because, although they are in their antecedents, their families, their experiences, part of all the crowds that follow Jesus, they are also separate. They have made, perhaps without even thinking about it very much, a total commitment and the working out of their commitment is turning out to be a lot more difficult than they expected. They, therefore, need to be reassured. They also need to be reminded of the importance of what they are doing. What they are doing is not just for them, but for all the people who look at them as the "little flock."

The kingdom is God's and God has chosen these people and God's promise is certain. It does not mean they should not attend to practical things. Rather, it is a call to feel free. It is a call to feel, yes, these things matter and we need to attend to them. Evidently there was a common purse and there were people who provided homes and places to stay and food--all these things matter. But let us not get so anxious about them that we lose sight of what we are really trying to do. It is not a kind of magic. God is not going to wave a wand to get rid of all earthly and material concerns. We have to think about these things. We have to take care. Rather, it is an attitude of mind. This "little flock" is the prophetic community, the one foretold by the prophets. It is the prophetic community in the sense that its very existence is a prophecy. Its attitude has to be one that recognizes this prophetic vocation. Everyday concerns of each person in the group are looked after in this context.

These people are called as a group, not only to announce as they go forth to share their message, but themselves to be an announcement. They are the announcement of God's reign. They have been chosen by God and, as people see them gathered around Jesus and see the way they live, they are to be in themselves proof of God's faithfulness, proof that God has not forgotten or left the people. But, because it was a close community and because there were people around Jesus who had a different attitude to possessions, the prophetic community in itself caused hostility and was going to cause hostility.

Jesus did not just preach. If he had confined himself to preaching, even as a prophet, probably he would not have aroused so much hostility. He might have provoked disagreement or perhaps disapproval, but not the intense, panicky hostility that clearly was aroused. This hostility came from the fact that Jesus put his words into practice, from the fact that he gathered around himself a different kind of community. This community was people who lived differently: people who cut through the social and religious cate-gories people had been taught to respect, people who should not have been together. Poor people and wealthy people, honest people ane people with dishonest backgrounds, men and women, all these were coming together, to listen together, to pray together, to eat together. The old accusation recurred, "he surrounds himself with sinners," with people who do not fit and who are not respectable. Some of them in fact were "respectable," but the point is that this judgment did not matter to Jesus. He was teaching the people with him that it did not matter. So there was this motley collection of people who very visibly followed him around. We recognize this motley crowd over and over in the gospels. In a society where, because of the climate, it was possible for people to be very visible when they were at meals it was quite noticeable that he had table fellowship with all kinds of people. This open table fellowship was an outrage to many.

Jesus called his "little flock" and established a messianic kingdom with these people. His "little flock" therefore looked different and, because it was different, it was very worrisome. These followers of his were people who were not afraid and not dependent. He was teaching them to be not afraid and not dependent. This sounds harmless, until you recognize that this society, like almost every other society that has ever been, was <u>built</u> on people being dependent and being afraid. People who make their money and who maintain their security by making sure other people are afraid and dependent are very frightened for themselves when the others who were dependent show signs of becoming independent. This independence frightens the people in power and makes them more punitive. It is the same in our society, for our society is also built on fear and dependence. People are dependent on their employers, on whether they are promoted, on whether they are sacked, on whether the whole place closes down. People are dependent on the welfare system and put up with the system's abuse, neglect, and refusal. People have no choice, having been trained all their lives, like women, to be dependent on men. In each case, the people in power are enraged if their dependents begin to show independence. They get very angry because they are themselves afraid and they will go to great lengths to suppress this independence, using physical violence, economic intimidation, verbal and emotional abuse. But Jesus had put courage and hope into people and had called them to be God's prophetic voice. This was extremely frightening in such a society. It rousecl anger and threat. It still does. It is, therefore, important to say "don't be afraid." Coupled with this is the need to sit lightly to possessions, accompanied by the promise that there would be treasure.

This does not mean, as I think many of those first followers of Jesus and many Christians since then have believed, that those who were faithful will get lots of possessions. It is rather that the treasure is a good thing, but that as things are held, used, and understood in a different way, their true value, the fact that they really are "treasure," is revealed. We do not normally think of things we use everyday as treasure, but this teaching of Jesus was calling people to recognize them as treasure, to recognize that the things that we use, the things we take care of, the things we share with each other, have this extraordinary value.

Perhaps the deepest indication of this treasure-like quality of ordinary things comes from a long tradition of the symbolism of the bread and wine Jesus shared at the Last Supper, a symbolism Christians have continued to share through the ages. Bread and wine are ordinary things, basic forms of food, and yet they have become symbols of the treasure God gives to each person and to the community. They are symbols of the treasure that, therefore, all earthly things are if used in the right way. The paradox is that, when people hang onto things and worry about them, they have, in a sense, no emotional freedom really to love the things they have. I think this call to let go of possessions and to give in charity is a call to recognize the treasure with which we have been entrusted. When you recognize the treasure, you will want to share it.

The prophetic community is paradoxical. First of all, it must, as I suggested earlier, work to restore the earth to God and to God's people. It must value the gifts of God and care for them. But it also has to sit lightly with those possessions. Knowing the hostility of the powers of oppression and the greed, the community knows it may well lose some security, may well lose possessions, may well be persecuted. On the one side, we are called to treasure what God gives and to share it because it is something to treasure. On the other, we are ordered not to hang on because if you do you may lose it. There are many people--not only the great martyrs of our time and of the past--but more ordinary people who have risked their jobs and, at a more bearable level, have taken a cut in salary for conscience's sake, who know what matters most and know they do receive treasure when they let go because they received a deeper quality of life.

So the hostility of the powers of oppression and greed threaten the ordinary livelihood of people who choose to accept the calling to be a "little flock." But there is something more. I said earlier that the existence of what Jesus calls his "little flock" is itself part of the proclamation. It is a prophetic community, not just in what it says but in what it is, and so its way of life is part of that proclamation. Its pattern of sharing and it simplicity of concern for each one is referred to by Jesus when he says, "Sell your possessions and give in charity." Make your treasure a common treasure. This is not just giving in charity in the sense of giving away, a bit of surplus, but the attitude of mind that says, "This is what God gives us, so we share it." This is what provides an unfailing treasure in heaven: the way that people live together; their lifestyles; their attitude toward things, which makes God's gifts visible treasure.

In the past, many Christians have treated abstemiousness as a virtue in itself. But I think what we sense here and in many other passages of the gospel is that virtue is in sharing and enjoying together what is given. The prophetic community grows out of the great prophetic announcements of the reign of God. It is a community that does have good things. It is not a community of want, but a community of common plenty. The vision of God's is a vision of enough for all.

What Jesus is telling us in Luke's vision and in many places is that it is truly possible for people to live together in harmony and for the earth to bring forth a plenteous harvest. There is enough for all, but never enough for greed. The letting go of greed makes us able to share, able to share the things we have and still have enough. I think at this time in human history this is much more literally obvious than it has been before. We recognize the choice of simplicity in lifestyle is not a particular virtue Christians may choose because it makes them feel good. The choice of simplicity in lifestyle is a necessity of survival. If we choose the gospel standard, if we choose to live as gospel people in simplicity and in sharing, we are simply doing what is required for the salvation of the earth, literally. For us to continue to have the earth as a home, there is never enough for greed. There <u>is</u> enough for the treasure God gives us.

There is enough if people will live in the way that respects what is given and, above all, in a way that respects each person. The condition of the reign of God is letting go. The reign of God seems to us so slow in coming. This is not because God is not eager to give it, but because we are very uneager to allow it to happen. We have to let go of acquisitiveness and of fear. We have to learn to care for the earth together and to share its good things. This can be done.

Jesus is telling us we should not fear that we are the "little flock," that we are in our small groups--in an apparently unimportant way--something very important: we are the prophetic sign, the prophetic voice, if we live as Jesus calls us to live. We have "a never failing treasure in heaven" that builds us up into a new way of being together. Nothing can destroy this except ourselves.

Where our treasure is, there our hearts will be also. Our treasure is God's gift of life and all the things that are part of life. Our treasure is the awareness of our intense interdependence, not only with each other, but with all created life, and of the responsibility for this. "Sell your possessions and give in charity," let go, but then receive. "It is your Father's pleasure." God's pleasure is to give us things, to give us the kingdom in which people are brothers and sisters to each other, in which people are like that early community around Jesus. God's pleasure is to give us the Kingdom in which people are astonished to find themselves snatched out of a way of life and thinking to which there never seemed to be any alternative and introduced to a whole new understanding of what life is about. This is very exciting and very frightening.

We are challenged all over again, as happens so often, each time we read scripture and allow ourselves really to feel it. We are challenged to recognize the extraordinary fact that it is God's pleasure, God's delight, God's joy to give us things. And so, in a sense, our way of life is based on the idea that it is our delight, our joy, our pleasure to share with each other, to share the earth, and our treasure, to take joy in all the things we have and in our relationships with each other.

Of course, we cannot do this all the time because a great deal of our life is anxious and struggling. We have constantly to listen again and hear, "Have no fear, don't be afraid." God says here, you are the "little flock," you are the ones chosen, and your chosenness and your togetherness is God's promise, is God's proclamation. This is, once more, the prophetic community. The community's common life is its proclamation. This is a tremendous responsibility. It is also a great reassurance since in a way it is very simple. We have each other. We tell each other what we need to do. We need not be afraid. We can share. There is enough. If persecution comes and if we lose things, there will be other people who can help us.

And so the reign of God, which is still to come, is yet already here, is already at work, is already apparent in the gathering of Christians, in the gathering of people of faith and good will who are willing to live into its Way. "Don't be afraid." We do have a treasure and it is God's pleasure that we have it.

GOD'S HOMECOMING
(Revelation 21:1-4)

This afternoon I want to offer my last contribution by reflecting on two things that struck me as I have heard what has been said here. The first has to do with the concerns for spirituality, for what spirituality might mean. The second comes out of the concern for spirituality because of the way in which we have used the word spirituality in the past: I have been wondering about the difference between heaven and earth and about what we mean by the kingdom of God. What has this to say to us as we make immediate practical decisions? It seems to me the sense of spirituality comes into this very strongly. Of course, this reflects my own personal predilection, which I am sure you recognize. But, after all, I can only offer you my own response and my own reaction, my own thoughts, and hope they will create a dialogue within yourselves.

What then is spiritual renewal? What is spiritual? I suppose one way to begin to think about this is to say what is spiritual is what is according to the spirit of God, the spirit poured out in Jesus and the spirit he affirmed and shared. This spirit was something that did not belong to him as a possession, but which Jesus was constantly recognizing, eliciting in people, calling upon people to accept and act out of: a bond of unity. Jesus seems to have been sure that everyone who heard him--if only they could hear clearly enough--could live out of the same spirit and, as it says in John's gospel, do the things that he did and even greater things: a staggering text if we think about it.

In the text from Revelation, the same idea comes through to me. God is here abolishing the distance between heaven and earth. The holy city, the human community, comes down from heaven, but comes down to earth. We are not told at any point that it goes back up again. We have very often thought of our relationship as a community of churches with God as that of people trying as best we can to discern God's word, share God's word, live out of it and codify it to whatever extent is necessary so everybody can understand it. I think there is a sense in which we will always have to do these things, because we struggle in at least semi-darkness to understand how we stand in relation to God. And yet this text, and so much else coming through to us from the prophets and from the gospel, seems to be saying something different. The heavenly community is rooted in the earth and, as in the reading from Jeremiah, God writes the law in the hearts of the people: people on earth.

The reign of God is, therefore, about transforming human experience. What then about heaven? What about this final transformation? We believe in the promise of a final transformation and, although we do not understand how it can happen, we have the great symbols of transformation. Many of the great symbols are in the book of Revelation. Moreover, we know of many people in Christian history who have had flashes of revelation. Perhaps some such people have come into our lives. There have been mystical experiences and extraordinary visions that have given momentary insight into the ultimate reality we believe will take over earthly experience. These mystical moments of vision are what T.S. Eliot called "moments out of time."

But we have to ask a very practical question: how does our earthly experience relate to this vision? How do we get from here to there? Do we just sit and wait for God to intervene? Is there something we have to do? The Gospels, the words of the prophets, and the words reverberating through Christian history, tell us that we are called to do something about it. We cannot bring about total transformation, but we are called to make it possible for this transformation to happen. We are so called because it seems that in all God's dealing with human beings, human beings, in a sense, have the last word. We can block divine love. This is the terrifying truth and it is a terrifying responsibility. So we are called to begin the work of total transformation, to begin to open the hearts, to open the doors, so that God can come in. It is finally God's work, but we human beings have to make it possible.

There is a phrase that became fashionable in theology some years ago--"realized eschatology"--a phrase meaning that the kingdom of God is still to come and yet is also already happening. And the fact is that we do already experience the reign of God. There are already times when we know we are engaged in something that is absolutely right, something that somehow resonates in our whole being. I imagine that for many people in the Church of the Brethren experience in volunteer service has been one of these experiences. These experiences can come to people in times of shared prayer or in the sense of having touched into something that gives us the feeling we know who we are, and what life is about. Such experiences give us a new energy. Such experiences can come at big shared moments, for instance when you take part in a big demonstration, when you are part of a movement with thousands of other people and you know what you are struggling for is worthwhile, that it is what God wants. In these moments there is tremendous liveliness, a tremendous sense of community that enables you to recognize this kind of community is at least potentially able to break down incredible barriers between people.

Such experiences also come in the small moments having a similar quality. I remember one such small moment in the early years of working at Wellspring House. A woman came to us, a woman who had been on the streets most of her life. A woman who had been abused and rejected since early childhood. She finally found some kind of lodging, then the house burned, and so she came to us with nothing but a plastic bag full of clothes that somebody had given her to replace her own clothes that had all burned. We discovered the date of her birth. This is one of those things we are supposed to put down on intake documents. As it happened, a few weeks later, it was her birthday. I asked her what kind of cake she liked. She said chocolate. So we made her a chocolate cake. We put candles on it and she cried because nobody had ever celebrated her birthday before. In this moment, we felt we shared a moment when you know the kingdom of God is indeed already reality.

There are many small moments; there are big moments. We know. Sometimes when we sing together we know. I referred earlier to the singing that we have shared together here. And I said to Lauree and Melanie, that this singing reminds me of a Welsh pub! This comparison is not as superficial or as funny as it sounds, since the tremendous Welsh tradition of singing comes from the chapel tradition of congregations too small and too poor to afford an organ. The Welsh people learned to sing a capella and to sing with great joy. If you go to a Welsh pub, even now-a-days, someone will suddenly begin to sing and everyone will pick it up, singing in several different parts. The Welsh also sing like this at football matches. There is a moment as people sing together when somehow barriers are broken and everyone knows something has been broken through. In these little and big ways, in so many ways--in times of worship, times of meeting, times of grief and loss--we may encounter a quality of rightness, of goodness we cannot question.

There is a lightness that comes from people in these moments. The only word to describe it is joy and joy is surely a mark of the reign of God. This recognition is beyond argument. You can take these moments apart, you can try to understand what happened and why it was important, but the experience itself is its own. And so we pray out of these moments to find a vision that may take on the whole earthly situation and begin to give it this kind of quality. It seems to me that in moments such as these, in moments when we know the spirit of God is present, the reign of God is truly here.

These moments sometimes offer us a touchstone. They tell us when we are headed in the right direction. They help us to allow God to be truly at home with us. At last God is with humankind, as the author of Revelations said. God is present and we know it.

How can we use these moments? We can do things and we can judge our progress by whether these moments happen. But there is more than this. The quality of behavior or of relationships or of whatever made these moments so special, is the standard by which we judge what we are doing. How can we, as Christians, hope to maximize and increase times like these, so God can come home more and more?

What we are looking for is a whole vision of what earthly companionship can be: the companionship of messianic fellowship. There are some very simple, basic human things promised by the prophets that were also promised by Jesus, and are at the heart of our effort to transform our world. These things are very, very simple, basic things: food; companionship; homes; work; health; a fertile and healthy earth. If we look at these things, I think we find a whole spirituality emerges.

Let us look first at food. A lot of our food now-a-days is grown in situations where the soil is drenched in toxic pesticides or with fertilizers that worry doctors because they feel that the soil producing our food lacks the minerals and nutrients we need. Food is produced in unsuitable places because in this way money can be made. For instance, we are pouring out our limited resource of water, by the millions of gallons, to grow crops that are not right for the kind of places where they are grown. And food is grown by underpaid people who have to work in dangerous conditions, who have to inhale toxic chemicals, because this is the only work they can find. The profits from all of this go to very large businesses and to very large corporations.

But it does not have to be like this. Food can be grown as it used to be--in organically tended soil and in mixed farms. Food can be grown by people who come together as individual farmers and by workers who come together in cooperatives or federations to help each other. Working together, healthy food can be produced and people can make a reasonable profit from it. Then the people who produce the food are also among the people who eat it. We have a symbol of this in the Lord's sharing of bread and wine at the Last Supper. This table fellowship was the mark of the messianic kingdom.

"Companionship" means the relationship among those who share bread and wine. It is a biblical symbol, as food is a biblical symbol of the messianic community. Perhaps we have to begin here. Perhaps we have to look at how we grow our food, how we buy our food, what food we buy. Perhaps we have to look at whether the people who are growing food are getting good wages and whether we can do something about this. We can, whether our action is a local or national boycott or whether it is simply encouraging our local stores to carry good food.

Then there are homes. Do we have to have an open market for homes, so that homes are a consumer commodity, so that the person with the most money gets the home? Is home ownership a luxury, and homelessness and insecurity the norm? Or can we envisage a society in which home ownership becomes the norm, in which we can offer people security whether they rent or own? This can be done with cooperatives where people help to build each other's homes. This can be done with "sweat equity" or some of the many other ways in which affordable homes are possible. This is a biblical concept. The idea of the "jubilee" is the idea that the earth does not belong to private individuals. The earth belongs to the whole people of God, since it is God's gift, and it should be returned to the people. This is a difficult concept for us, but it is actually a very practical one. One of the things that Wellspring House has done is to set up a "land trust," which is one of the ways affordable housing can become accessible.

These are the things people can do locally without delay. These are means to new possibilities the Bible demands. These are things that can be done. The reign of God can be established to this extent. God can come into people's life as they discover the self-respect having their own home can bring them.

What about work, employment? For most people, it is a matter of surviving. You take whatever work you can get and you worry about whether you will have it next week. People are just hands to produce, and they are replaceable by machinery. People can be exploited and, almost literally, enslaved. Big corporations move their factories out of this country, where they would have to pay at least minimum wage, to Third World countries, where people can be paid whatever the corporation chooses to pay them to work in atrocious conditions with no safety precautions. I heard one representative of a corporation saying that it is ok to employ women in Korea and in other Third World countries to do incredibly minute, very repetitive work at starvation wages, since, in his words, that is all they are used to doing. Work does not have to be like this. In many places there are work cooperatives. There are also employee-managed businesses. There are small businesses that help each other through small local banks. There are all kinds of ways people have already found to make work something that can be good and full of dignity and hope. And there are ways people have already found to make work something that can produce things people really need, because one of the problems in our time is that a great amount of work produces things nobody needs and everybody would be far better off without.

We can begin at the local level, in small ways, to make these changes. We can buy from firms that have a just employment policy. We can join or support worker's cooperatives, to make it possible for people to know such things exist.

What about health? The so-called "health" business is really an illness business. It is high-tech medicine at a very high cost. Less and less medical insurance coverage is available. Some people do not have any and have never had any. Moreover, when things get difficult and there is a deficit, states cut back on medical services for the poor. Some people make a great deal of money on "health" services. It does not have to be like this. We can encourage local, ordinary, low-tech health education and health care in local communities. This takes money, but not an awful lot; it can be done. We need to train people in home nursing care so that the sick can be taken care of in their own homes when they come out of the hospital or so they can avoid going to the hospital altogether. We need to train people to teach others basic nutrition so they can keep healthy.

These sorts of neighborhood health and nursing care used to be the norm; they could be again.

And what about our environment? We are very, very conscious of environmental concerns now. There are strong biblical roots for this, concern for all of creation because we are all created beings. Even the ox trampling around to separate the grain is not supposed to be muzzled because, after all, he has a right to some of the produce of his own labor. And there is the injunction that fields should be rested. There is a sense that we are a part of an intricate network of created beings. There is a sense that all of us depend on every other one.

We can do quite a lot about this interdependence, even as individuals. We can cut back on waste. We can stop buying things we do not need. We can try as far as possible to buy well-made things that are produced without toxic processes and without toxic wastes. We can use biodegradable cleaning products. We can recycle locally. We can use less. We can take canvas bags when we go to shopping instead of getting more and more plastic or paper bags for carrying our groceries. We can set up a local furniture barn where volunteers repair and restore furniture and appliances for people who cannot afford new ones. This would mean people without would have what they need and it would mean old furniture and appliances would not end up in the dump. We can plant trees, more and more trees. We can join environmental groups that protest the destruction of nature. We can make gardens, even in the middle of cities. There are already many city gardens, beautiful little oases in the middle of asphalt where people can share the work of producing their own food. These are symbols of something new and different.

All this practical stuff, all this very nitty-gritty stuff, emerges from a vision, a biblical vision. Doing it, doing it--actually taking the trouble to get together and do it--creates deep spiritual change, even if we begin without a profound understanding of its spiritual importance. Actually doing it together means that we take on a different attitude in relation to each other, a different attitude in relation to the earth, a different attitude in relation to God. It is a whole spirituality we learn as we share in these simple, basic human concerns, because these are concerns about God's gifts to us, about how to use them, and about how not to abuse them.

If we want spiritual renewal, here is the possibility. This practical stuff deepens our awareness of what our treasure is. It helps us to find freedom from attachment and also from insecurity. It helps us to build community because nearly all of these things are things we have to do together. So we educate ourselves and we educate each other. Together we come to a new awareness of each other as stewards of God's creation.

There is another thing that happens. Doing this kind of thing can remain very local, but even at the local level it requires strong cooperation and organization if it is going to be done well. You cannot just rush into this kind of thing and hope it is going to turn out all right. You have to have skills. You have to learn. You have to understand how it is done and how to organize for it. But, in many cases, it will immediately demand something wider as well. It will demand cooperation at the state or even the national level. This practical stuff will bring us in touch with other people's efforts in the same direction so we are able to draw on their experience and share experience with them, so we are able to understand what other people are doing and to learn from them and teach them. A wider and wider network is thereby created. We learn different ways of working together and we correct these ways whenever they are not efficient. If they do not help us to do what we set out to do, we realize they are not going in the right way and so we have to find another. What we are doing, really is experimenting with different kinds of human structure at the same time we are doing these simple things God calls us to do. We are finding ways to be together as God's people, new ways.

These human structures are spiritual because they are the direct outcome of our response to the spiritual call to transform the earth, to make "a new heaven and a new earth." Insofar as we allow God's reign to take over our actions and our decisions, the city of God comes down to earth and, in some places and in some ways, the mourning and the pain cease and the tears are wiped away. This seems small and the old order is very strong. The old order will not give in easily. It has been around a long time and is very skilled at survival. Only God knows how long the struggle may be and how much grieving we still have to do for the evil in the world and for our own failure. But, insofar as we obey the calls of the prophets and of Jesus, insofar as we obey the silent word of God in our hearts and the word of God we discover among ourselves, the old order has given way.

We experience this transformation in the symbols given to us in the passage. We read of a wedding, a party, a celebration. When we encounter these moments we are certain this is what the reign of God is all about. We recognize these moments because of the joy and because the prophetic symbol for this kind of joy is the wedding party, the messianic banquet. It is the prophetic vision of a banquet to which everyone is invited. But some people get a special invitation. These people are the ones who are least likely to be invited to any of the banquets we normally hear about: the poor; the oppressed; the alienated; the angry; the sick; the despairing; the rejected; the abused. And, simply statistically, we have to remember the majority of these people are women. Women receive a special invitation to this banquet. The banquet is the symbol of plenty. You do not give a banquet if you have only enough to manage; you give a banquet because you have a lot to share. It is the plenty of a world restored to health, able to provide healthy and plentiful food for the people who have the freedom to come together in joy.

A long time ago, in the fourteenth-century, there was a woman whose name we do not even know. We know her only by the name she took when she became an anchoress or hermit living in a two-room cell attached to the wall of the church of St. Julian. We call her Julian of Norwich. She lived through the kind of horror and turmoil we are experiencing in many parts of the world today. She lived through the time of the Black Death. Three times during her early life this plague came and half of the population of the country died in pain and horror. She also lived through the time of the peasant's revolt, when people oppressed beyond bearing rose up under the standard of the gospel to claim their rights as human beings and were betrayed, punished, hanged and tortured. You would think that these experiences would be enough to give anybody a rather dark view of human life. And yet when you read her book of the Revelations of Divine Love, you would never guess these circumstances were the background of her writing. But she knew these circumstances since the people who lead the peasant's revolt came from her part of the country. Indeed, she experienced the revolt first hand. She also, in her revelations, encountered the suffering Christ first hand. And, through her experience, she began to understand that God's will is not evil and pain, but is goodness and love. At one point she was shown what she called "a little thing the size of a hazel nut" and it seemed to her that this little thing was "all it is." It was so small and insignificant she wondered why it did not fall apart. She was told that God cares for it and so it will not fall apart. It is safe. At the end of her book, she repeats the lines that have become so familiar, lines that have come out of her terrible background of experience of shared pain. In the midst of so much pain, she assures us that "all shall be well, all shall be well, and all manner of things shall be well."[3]

It is very hard for us to believe these lines. If we come through a time of grieving and repentance, if we come through the time of puzzlement, confusion, and anxiety, if we are tempted to rely on changing this little bit and that little bit, we can be challenged by the pain and the suffering around us, we can be challenged by the goodness we experience. We can recognize the goodness as the presence of God. Julian asked in her vision "What is God's meaning?" She was told, "Love [is] his meaning." This is why, despite everything or perhaps through everything, we can say, "all shall be well and all shall be well and all manner of thing shall be well."

CHAPTER THREE

CALLING TO MINISTRY IN THE CHURCH OF THE BRETHREN

Robert E. Faus

The Church of the Brethren has historically been a part of the family of "believers'" churches that stress the "priesthood of all believer's" or the ministry of every baptized person. Building on this foundational understanding of ministry the church has called people as a way of identifying gifts for leadership in ministry. A recent survey, part of the Lilly Endowment grant process, asked congregations to indicate their present understanding and practice of calling. They were asked whether they identify themselves as calling congregations and, if so, how they carry out this mission in their corporate life? What follows is a summary of the responses to this survery's questions.

The Process

Church of the Brethren district executives from each of the twenty-four districts nominated a broad, representative range of congregations, taking into consideration such factors as size, location, style of ministry (full-time, part-time, multiple staff, free ministry), age of members, and theological perspectives. One hundred nine congregations received the questionnaire; thirty-seven of them returned it. The congregations who responded constituted a representative sample of the spectrum of congregations that received the survey.

Congregations were asked to indicate their understanding of four different, although related, definitions of calling by responding to these questions:

1. Is calling each member's acceptance of responsibility for the ministry of the church at her or his baptism? Is

this understanding of calling taught and nurtured in the congregation?

2. Is calling the ways by which persons are chosen for leadership in the congregation?

3. Is calling the way in which gifts for set-apart ministry are recognized and congregational initiative in recommending such persons to districts for licensing and ordination are carried out?

4. Is calling the way in which a pastor is secured for a congregation?

Congregations were invited to elaborate on the third and fourth of these definitions. With regard to calling persons to set-apart ministry, congregations told stories about the nature of their local experience with such calling and about persons who were called. They indicated frequency, criteria and qualities relative to calling, showing how they support persons they call. With regard to calling pastors, congregations were asked to identify factors that helped them know certain pastors were right for them and to recall particular gifts for ministry that contributed to good and to poor "fits" between pastors and congregations.

Congregational Use of Calling

According to the survey responses, calling is least used to define congregational processes for obtaining local leadership. Respondents speak of electing, voting, and balloting; they seldom connect such processes to calling. Similarly, there seems to be little connection between calling and the assumption of ministry by every member at baptism. In fact, only a few responding congregations give any indication of support for this theological conviction. Thirty-one respondents affirm the congregation's role of calling persons to the set-apart ministry. The remaining six answered the questions in this section of the survey solely with reference to calling a pastor. Clearly, there is a need to rekindle awareness of the foundational relationship of the universal ministry to the role of the congregation relative to calling.

Ten of the total sample cannot recall ever calling anyone to ministry, even though most of them feel it is part of the congregation's role. Those who have called persons did so some time ago (over thirty years) or only relatively recently (in the last ten years). The responding congregations called no one from the beginning of the 1960s until the middle of the 1970s.

Approximately seventy persons were called by the twenty-seven congregations who indicated they had extended calls. The responses suggest a high level of acceptance of the call, resulting in the assumption of pastoral leadership and ongoing recognition of these pastors by the congregations that called them. Congregations who have called persons to set-apart ministry have a sense of satisfaction about having done so.

A dramatic change has taken place in the church with regard to who initiates or who is the agent of the call. This change was highlighted in responses to the survey. Historically, congregations, whose members were all considered to be part of the church's ministry, called forth or elected some from among themselves to be leaders. Even though deacons, elders and official boards may have had a formative role in nurturing such leaders, the congregations clearly took the initiative in naming and calling persons. The congregations acted out of the conviction that the Holy Spirit was at work among them in this calling process.

Yet seventeen of the responding congregations in the survey name individual initiative as the primary factor leading to a call to ministry. Although other agents of call are mentioned--such as the pastor, a congregational leader, church board or committee--the congregation as calling agent is not mentioned. One consequence of this change is that congregations have often become the responders to individual initiative in the calling process. The only exception to this change in patterns of calling is found in several free ministry congregation where practices remain consistent with the traditional congregational role.

Finally, the survey shows that the clearest, most commonly accepted understanding of the congregational role in calling is calling pastors. All congregations, again with the exception of the free ministry congregations, report a familiarity with their role in responding to a need for pastoral leadership. This is to say, they understand the pastoral search process and have an awareness of the needed gifts for ministry.

The responses received from this sampling are, of course, not definitive for all congregations. Still, some patterns emerging from the responses raise several concluding questions about the congregations' understanding of calling and of their role in extending calls to persons. Has the Church of the Brethren narrowed the focus of the call in restrictive and self-defeating ways, especially in light of traditional practices? If so, why has this narrowing taken place? Does the search for quality leadership in the church require a more assertive calling practice by congregations? Has the transition from free ministry by multiple persons in a particular congregation to a professional model of pastoral ministry effected a change in congregational understandings and exercises of calling?

Qualities for Ministry

Congregations were asked to identify qualities they sought in persons they called to ministry, in persons they called as pastors, as well as in the pastors they remember positively. A comparison of the qualities that were named in these regards is significant and revelatory.

As might be expected in a church with a strong emphasis on the gathered faith community, the ability to relate well to people of varying ages and personalities is highly desirable. The ability to preach, whether perceived as a spiritual gift or a professional skill, is also very much desired in persons being called to the set-apart ministry or to serve a congregation or both. Brethren also agree quite clearly that personal commitment and dedication to the calling are crucial for those they call and for those who lead congregations. Along with this dedication is a desire for sincerity and faithfulness in persons who serve in the set-apart ministry. Brethren are most likely to seek to discern these qualities in issuing a call to persons or in employing persons for pastoral leadership. Given the strong agreement on these qualities in the responses, it seems that for Brethren relational abilities, preaching skills and sincere commitment to the call are the most valued qualities for ministry.

Personality and character are also significant and commonly agreed considerations in issuing a call either to enter ministry or to serve a congregation. Akin to the relational skills more specifically named above, personality characteristics favored in those whom Brethren call and in those they employ as pastors include honesty, open-mindedness, listening skills, ability to involve others in the ministry of the congregation and the ability to relate to the community in which the congregation is located.

Other factors mentioned are the candidate's theological position, and, to a minimal degree, interest in evangelism. The significance of the theological position in the responses did not indicate a kind of theology, but was concerned that the theological position of the candidate matched the congregation's. In other words, the congregation does not seem to care as much about what the candidate believes as whether her or his beliefs will work well with the congregation's belief system.

Some of the contrasts between qualities desired in calling and qualities remembered relative to good pastors are startling. For example, the candidate's own interest and desire to be called is strongly desired for issuing a call (consistent with the earlier results that names individual initiative as the most common way of issuing a call). But in remembering those who served well, the pastor's personal sense of being called by God is mentioned only once. The congregation's sense that the person is led by the Holy Spirit, perhaps a related quality, is mentioned only twice. While individual initiative seems to be very important for Brethren to consider issuing a call currently, and seems to be the leading way our denomination does call at present, it is insignificant in what is valued and remembered relative to good pastors.

Moreover, leadership (never defined or elaborated in any of the responses) is also an important quality in issuing a call or employing a pastor. It is mentioned twelve times by congregations. But it is remembered as a quality of a good pastoral relationship only half as many times. Similarly, the candidate's spirituality (also never defined or elaborated in responses) is a quality discerned in issuing a call, but lifted up as a memorable quality of a good pastor only half as often. A strong sense of Brethren identity is significant among those Brethren who call someone into the set-apart ministry. But, again, only about half as often is this remembered as one of the features of someone who served well.

Teaching is not nearly as important to good pastoral relationships as it seems to be in discerning candidates to call into ministry. Seminary training is important to a limited degree in those who are called to pastor a congregation, but it is even less a factor in making for a good pastor-congregational match.

There are some other startling contrasts between the qualities named as contributions to a good pastoral fit, and those mentioned as qualities congregations look for in calling persons to ministry or to the pastorate. Administrative ability is a well-remembered quality, but it is named as a gift discerned for issuing a call only one-third as often. Visitation and pastoral counseling are overwhelmingly named as important for a good pastor-congregation relationship, but are almost not named as traits sought in calling out ministers or searching for a pastor. More interesting is the naming (seventeen times) of a caring and loving personality as contributing significantly to good pastoral relationships with congregations, while naming these same personality characteristics as important to discern among candidates for the call less than one-third as often. A similar surprise occurs as a good pastor is frequently (sixteen times) named as feeling like a part of the congregational family, while this sense of belonging is never named as an important quality among those being considered for a call.

Congregations highly value pastors who are caring and loving and who visit among the membership. They treasure a feeling of relatedness between pastor and congregation that is as close as family ties. These qualities are named as hallmarks of good pastors. But these are not articulated nearly as well among the qualities congregations try to discern in issuing a call into set-apart ministry or pastoral leadership.

Concluding Reflections

It could be happy coincidence or the work of the Holy Spirit that brings together the church's renewed interest in calling, especially on the part of the congregation, and an emerging concern for sufficient quality leadership. The gifts of the congregational leaders, who contributed their own experience of calling to the wider conversation of the church, and of the district executives, who cared about this and other portions of these special denominational explorations of ministry to offer their gifts of administration and insight, are much appreciated.

CHAPTER FOUR

IN THEIR OWN WORDS: STORIES OF CALLING AND FORMATION

John J. Cassel

Concern for calling and leadership development is not new to the Church of the Brethren. Minutes of Annual Conferences evidence that already thirty years ago there was recognition of a problem and there were attempts to find more functional patterns of calling and sustaining ministers. The issues of quality and quantity were both present. Many of the factors influencing ministry have not changed dramatically. Thus it is especially interesting to hear the stories of persons representing a broad range of ages.

The following stories of ordained ministers in the Church of the Brethren, stories of persons across a broad age range, bring the issues of calling and leadership development to life. They connect generalized understandings of ministry to the concrete experiences of real people.

Data Collection

In the fall of 1988, I conducted twenty-seven telephone interviews with set-apart leaders in the Church of the Brethren. These leaders were asked to talk about their own ministry and the path by which they came to ministry. Candidates for these interviews were identified by asking District Executives to name "quality persons" in a number of categories: graduates of Bethany Theological Seminary, "free" ministers; graduates of other seminaries; and retired ministers.

Organizing Themes Arising from the Data

l) The initiative in calling. Given the Church of the Brethren's "free" ministry heritage, it is interesting to observe where the initiative for ministry originates. Does it come from the congregation and church members or does it come from within the candidate?

2) Early experiences in ministry and leadership. There is a striking emphasis on the early ministry experiences of persons who later became ordained leaders. These persons were asked to assume leadership and ministry roles and were affirmed in those roles.

3) The role and status of ministry within our contemporary church and society is a mixed picture. A number of the interviewees experienced ministry as upward mobility. Others speak about the overwhelmingly complex set of demands currently placed on pastors. Still others talk about the "kept" nature of pastoral ministry in our time.

4) The vitality and life of the church. If the church is exciting and things are happening, people will choose to invest themselves in significant ways. What do variations in congregational vitality mean in the context of calling? What does it mean to now be in a time of diminishing membership and resources?

Preliminary Analysis of the Interviews

1) Gender: Seven of the twenty-seven interviewees were women. Of the Bethany graduates, none of the ten quality persons identified from 1961-75 were women. In contrast, four of the five quality persons identified from 1981-85 were women.

2) Age and the initiative for ministry:

Age	No.	Congregational initiative	Both Self & Congregation	Self Alone
60-77	4	25%	75%	-0-
50-59	8	38%	75%	25%
40-49	7	28%	71%	28%
28-39	8	25%	28%	62%

3) Five persons report no hindrances to be overcome as they moved into ministry. All were over 48 years of age, 31% of those over 48. Of the Bethany graduates, only those who graduated before 1965 reported a smooth glide into ministry.

4) Six persons spoke about direct personal experience of God's calling. All these persons were over 50 years of age.

In Their Own Words

The following are quotations from the interviews, quotations that move from one particular point of view to another.

Experience and Affirmation in Ministry

"When I was a high school senior, they said I should be assistant Sunday School superintendent. But I said I couldn't get up and say a prayer or speak in front of people. But they kept encouraging and I did it. And then they said they needed a teacher for the young adult class (the one I felt was the hardest to teach.) There was no way I could do this. But they kept encouraging me . . . (later) I felt I wanted to do more . . . . I thought that I might be able to preach part-time. So I talked to the pastor and he said why don't you think about being licensed."

"My assignments in summer pastorates during my junior and senior years at Bridgewater, coupled with pretty high level of satisfaction in debate, confirmed my desire to continue toward seminary at the first opportunity.

"So I started taking religion classes mainly out of pure curiosity and interest and loved them. . . . My first summer in college I went back to find a job and ended up working at McDonalds and was very unhappy. So the next summer I did summer service with a program at LaVerne College and went to Bakersfield and loved it. The Bakersfield church wrote a letter to my home congregation and said we see gifts in that person for ministry and we'd really like to see you consider licensing her."

"I just can't say enough for the small church. They kind of took me under their wing even though I was very green and inexperienced and they loved me and cared for me and cared for our family and helped us in a million ways. I ended up having fifteen funerals there in the three years I was there. Most of them stalwarts of the church. I really came to grips with what is life all about."

"I went down to the work camp and that's when I thought seriously about ministry and I came home and told Bob Hess about it. He told me that I would have to go on to college."

"My senior year in high school was another turning point for me. I was rather timid and shy and had a low self esteem. Yet I was listed on the ballot to be our youth president (along with some key people in our group) . . . and I was the one elected to be the youth president! That became a very important challenge to me. And the more I worked at that, the more it became clear that I possibly had some skills and gifts that the church might want to use."

Congregational Life

"The Youth Group was always pretty important. National Youth Conference was always a real important event in my life. Growing up in a pastor's family gave me a real sense of security and stability and having a family who worshipped together. I complained a lot about being in a pastor's family, but in a lot of ways it was a real gift to me.

"I experienced support and encouragement from my wife and my parents, from a few friends in college, from one or two people at church. But, I never really received much support from the congregation as a whole. . . . In other words, they didn't call me but I offered myself because I sensed a call."

"The problem in my opinion, is not leadership development. The problem is the church. The church is in desperate, desperate straights. I mean the church. Not just the Church of the Brethren . . . I still think the church has probably the best chance of any institution in our culture to help care for and support people. But I can't in integrity sit down with someone and say 'You ought to be going into ministry'. I can't do that right now. I'd like to but I can't do it with integrity or enthusiasm. It takes a lot of education to become a minister and then you're not going to be paid well. It's going to be tough on family and spouse. The expectations are going to be stressful. On and on. You don't build enthusiasm by building a task force to build enthusiasm. You get your house in order and then people will be enthusiastic. We don't have a shortage of human beings. The issue is getting them attracted to something that can challenge their life that they see as fulfilling and exciting."

Spouses

"I don't think that I would have survived in the pastorate at times if (my wife) hadn't given me the kind of whole-hearted support she has given. The decision to go to Bethany, she whole-heartedly supported. I'm talking about support for my sense of call, too."

"I have the benefit of a wife who totally supports and compliments who I am as a pastor. Without that I am not sure I would be here today. I know some of my peers who don't have that and I know of the agony and struggles they go through because of that. That needs to be included in that preparation process towards pastoral ministry."

Family of Origin

"Certainly the support has been from my family. I think my mother really wanted me to go into parish ministry. I don't remember her ever saying that to me. I don't know that my Dad cared a great deal one way or the other. He cared about me and about what happened to me, but not what direction. Grandma thought it was the greatest thing since napkins!"

"I would have to begin with the fact that in my family tradition the church was the central focus of our lives except for family. And the set-apart ministry was held in very high esteem in my family. My Dad was not a minister, but my Granddad was and I had a half dozen uncles who were in the ministry."

"My Dad was a very active lay person. He was a teacher of a young adult class. There are a couple of persons who have told me that they were in ministry because of my Dad's influence in that class. He was the kind of person that took what he believed seriously in terms of living it out in active involvements in the community and in the church. He was the kind of person that was on the ministry board and youth Sunday School class and was there when the church was opened and stayed till it closed."

Youth Program

"Well, I remember specifically being triggered to think about full time Christian service at National Youth Conference. It was the second National Youth Conference at Estes Park. A sermon talked about the need for quality church leadership and giving our best and responding to God's gift to us by returning a year or two of full-time Christian service. And I remember at the end of this speech he said something like the call that came to Isaiah, "Who shall I send?" And then he invited us to commit one or more years of our life to Christian service to raise our hands. And I, along with several thousand other people, raised my hand. That was a powerful moment for me."

"We had an unusually large and active youth group at that time. It was kind of an exciting time. To have four of our group headed for ministry at the same time. We had about 30 in our youth group. And most of us sang in the choir. We had our youth meetings every Sunday evening just prior to Sunday evening service. It was an exciting and nurturing group."

"I suspect that started to grow on me at First National Youth Conference in 1954 in Anderson, Indiana hearing Bob Richards speak."

"I had a very meaningful evangelical type experience. And concurrent with that, since I had been about 9 years old, I had been going to church camp at Camp Harmony, but in those summer camp experiences there was a very strong emphasis on Christian service and youth at least considering the possibility of full-time Christian service. And in my home church, John Ellis took a very strong interest in approaching persons who he thought had gifts for ministry and encouraging them to consider that. So at any given time in the Moxham church we had several people licensed for ministry in apprentice kinds of roles."

"I don't remember too much about camp, but I remember the final campfire when we were to make some kind of commitment. And that spoke to me. It was this kind of influence, not something that happened all at one time, but it was a progression of prods from the Lord along the way over a period of years."

"There was in my home church a deep emphasis on seeking God's will not only in my career but in choosing my mate. God has a plan for your life and God has a mate for you. God has a choice and anything else is second best."

An Encouraging Elder

"I remember one Sunday morning, church was over and we were shaking hands at the door. He looked at me and he said as I went out the door, 'You know you ought to really consider the ministry.' So when my wife and I had sat down to eat dinner, she said to me '"What was T.G. talking to you about?"' 'Well, he put his arm around me and he said "You know you ought to really think about the ministry.' She looked at me and said, 'I think he's right.'"

"The lady who led the work camp was a dynamic kind of person. She was just a lay person but she was a strong person to encourage people and get them to look at their gifts and what they could do. Of course then at McPherson I remember M.R. Ziegler coming to campus. He met with us and encouraged us."

"I went to Juniata in the days of Charles Ellis. And he was a very strong person advocating a service ministry of some kind. Whether it was teaching or in some area of the church's ministry. And I heard that for four years at Juniata. And it apparently made an impression."

A Wise Mentor or Teacher

"There was a Dr. Edna Fells in Iowa and I wrote her and asked her if I could work out a plan where I could work with her for a summer. She was spectacular. I was there for three months under her and went with her on calling. I just was around all the time. We blocked out three hours of study time that was not debatable every morning of the week. And she studied in one room and I studied in the other and she gave me sermon topics and I had to provide fuel for her sermons. I'd hear her saying things in the pulpit that I had come up with. She was my mentor."

"The one that really left an impression was Dave Eiler. He was professor of religion and I enjoyed his classes. I was his assistant and got to correct some of his quizzes."

"I didn't set out to college with set-apart ministry in mind. In fact, I had some fancy thoughts that it might be medicine. But as I got into my subjects at college, particularly Bible and philosophy and sociology, my thoughts began to turn toward the church ministry or toward church service. And I got encouragement from the family and also from the local congregation and by mid-point of my sophomore year I was licensed."

"I was stimulated in one of Tim Rieman's classes and became interested in philosophy. His notion was that, if you're preparing for medical school, you take the necessary preparatory work. The same way in ministry. You don't prepare for the ministry by taking every other subject. So I followed that advice and transferred over to religion and philosophy major with the full intent of going to Bethany."

"I remember one person in my high school days that said 'You really don't want to go into ministry unless that's the only thing you can do'. In other words, unless the call is so strong that you, no matter what, have to go there. The person who cared about whether

I was going to be a pastor or not was Phil. He was never trying to fit me into a box. Never tried to force me. But he was a good listener. He was a good person to bounce off all of my stupid, dumb feelings, and check out some of my attitudes. He did that in a supportive, caring kind of way."

Heroes and Models

"I can remember at least two Sunday school teachers who were persons you looked up to and felt good about. Just the way they lived out their faith and the way they taught sort of gave encouragement. They were ones who encouraged me to do this."
"There's been a mystique around my grandfather. I've heard about him from my grandmother, from my mother, his daughter, and I've known about him from parishioners. Every one who has talked to me has held him in sort of a revered status."

"In this very fundamental church there was a very interesting pastor. He held to all of the fundamentals but he had such a loving nature about himself. He was very influential on my life as I grew up. He was the one who got me really turned on to social action, just because of the things he did. Caring for the poor, taking care of widows, doing things to help people. He was sort of a worker priest who went out and did carpentry work and other things and made a little money. I think he helped to develop within my mind what life ought to be about, which is serving and caring for people."

"I had a very positive image of pastors at that time. And it was mostly focused in one person: Harry Zeller. I was attracted to his style and the way he did ministry."

"As a teenager growing up I was very close to my home church pastor. I held him in very high esteem and found him to be very supportive of my own life and my own struggles. It was very easy to talk to him and I looked to him as being someone who helped to fulfill what ministry was all about."

The Free Ministry Setting

"In those days they asked members of the district ministry commission to come in and conduct the election. At that time these two men met in the back room and people filed through one at a time to cast their vote and I was elected to the ministry. That was the third of August 1943. I was about twenty-six, married, had children. I was a route supervisor for the Moore Dairy in Lancaster, Pennsylvania. I remember Forney who was moderator, after the meeting that night said, 'Earl, I want you to preach a week from Sunday.' I had no earthly idea about how to prepare a sermon."

"As the church has moved largely from the self-supported ministry to the full-time professional ministry, in most congregations there seems to be present very little activity in initiating the calling of people into the ministry. And it seems like many, many pastors find it awkward to lead a congregation to the point of actually calling somebody from the group to be a minister. I think that is one of the reasons we don't have that steady supply of ministers that the free ministry used to generate. I think some pastors feel threatened by it and others feel bothered that they have to work with a young minister. I think every congregation ought to go through a periodic, soul-searching calling among themselves to the ministry. It really has an effect on a congregation that takes the call seriously because everybody is a potential candidate and it causes everybody to do some soul-searching."

"I may have been the first minister at Chiques who indicated an interest in ministry before they took a vote. Now we've done it both ways since that time. Although I think there is still a hesitancy among some people to let it be known that they are considering ministry, I think we need to get to the place where both of those ways are just as valid as the other."

Specific Direct Experience Of Calling

"About the fourth or fifth night along the trail week when it was time for evening devotions, there was a terrific thunder storm. I loved those. We were sitting on the porch of this old cabin up in the mountains of Pennsylvania. Because of the noise of the thunder and the rain we couldn't even have the devotions that were prepared So we just kind of sat there and sang hymns. Well, part way through that night, all of a sudden I got the feeling that God was standing right behind me. That there was a presence so palpable that I can understand people in the Old Testament talking with God. It was just as clear as anything that I was called to ministry. And I remember at the time I stood up and told the rest of the group of my call and my response. Ray was the only one who responded out of the whole group. He said 'God bless you Bob' and I felt that Ray's blessing has kind of abided with me all these years."

"I went to Elizabethtown College to play sports and not to study and I wasn't getting along well in school. I wasn't studying very well, and went to a revival meeting at Meyerstown with Ralph Schlosser preaching. And I heard a call. And things turned around and I began to feel a sense of direction for my life."

"I think the real call that I had, occurred while I was in Korea. I remember it was colder than all get out and I had gotten awake to go on guard duty from about 2:00 to 4:00 in the morning. I remember out walking in the snow, cold and looking up into the heavens and almost saying 'O God, is this what life is all about?' I never had any voices talk to me but really felt the direct call to say, you really need to think about going back home and becoming one of my ministers."

"I had one of those divine call kinds of experiences in the midst of a struggle I had with depression following the birth of one of our children and a sense of call as I moved out of that experience. I sensed my call to be toward equipping persons for ministry to others."

"What I consider to be the call to ministry came to me when I was a sophomore in high school. I was in an assembly hall at the high school ready to take a history exam. And it came to me after the instructions had been given to not leave the room, it was impressed upon me, either by a voice or by a spirit, I'm not sure, to go to the church office and pray. I got up and left the room. Nobody questioned me. I went into the church office lounge, knelt down, and I can remember acknowledging that I didn't know what this was all about, and then being in prayer that I was to be either a missionary or minister. I rose from those moments of contemplation, went to the office phone and called a professor there at the college. I told him where I was and told him that I had experienced something very different and wondered if he could come to the school and talk to me. He came over and I told him what happened. He did not interrogate me. He did not overplay it. He simply said to me, 'Now if that be the call, then what you are to do is to go back in, finish your history exam, finish your high school, and prepare yourself to go to college.' We had a prayer and that was it."

The Licensing and Ordination Process

"The district was real supportive. I've heard of other people who've had difficult experiences with the Atlantic Northeast commission. I know that there are people on there who are pretty conservative toward women in ministry. Harold Bomberger was the person who did my licensing and then Earl Ziegler took over and he did the ordination. I have positive feelings toward the district. I didn't run into the typical obstacles that I might have."

"I was licensed half way through my first year of college--which was, I think, a considerable risk on the part of the district. I don't know why they did that. Ordination followed as a matter of fact.

Ordinarily and uninspiringly. In fact, somewhat discouragingly. After I graduated from seminary and knew I had a pastorate the ordination was disappointing. Neither of the two interviews really, I think, came to grips with me or my faith. And I still don't understand what the value of those interviews were for the people who did the interviewing. I've had a sort of sense of discomfort with that process."

"I really didn't have an understanding of what ought to be happening between the church and myself. There was a sense in which I felt that the call was so strong and so real and so authoritative, that I kind of short-circuited the business of the church. I really didn't need their approval . . .. The thing that I would have appreciated from my local congregation was to have them take initiative away from me. I'm not sure I would have liked it at the time. But I would have liked if my congregation had said 'We're glad that you feel this call inside. We respect that. But we ourselves as a congregation, we want to call you to ministry. This is our agenda. And whatever voices you may have heard, whatever call you may have heard, we want you to know that we, the Rocksbury Congregation, want to call you to be a minister.'"

"I remembered being interviewed by the Elders body and I remember them asking if I was going to insist on playing baseball when I was a minister. I said I didn't see any contradiction between the two. They said, 'Well how about playing baseball on Sundays?' And I said, 'Well I'm active in the church in the morning and I didn't see that it would detract any.' That didn't wash too well in the 1950s."

"In retrospect, I think my journey was too smooth. I wish I would have been more introspective. I'm not sure I would have made a different decision. I think I would have known more about where I was headed. Now how do we put that together with being seventeen."

Women in Ministry

"I went to seminary thinking 'I can't do this'. And I came out feeling like I could. Probably in part through Field Education. I went to the Summer Pastorate with a chip on my shoulder thinking they weren't going to like a woman in ministry. But that was my own issue more than anything. I find that it depends a lot on my attitude."

"I don't think that before I got to seminary I was brave enough to tell anybody that I wanted to be in the ministry. That just wasn't something I was ready to say and my home church of course had never had a woman who was interested in ministry. Nobody other than the pastor at my home church thought it was a sane idea."

"I think the sexual identification of ministry, particularly pastoral ministry with males, was a significant one for me. And I knew some women who had entered into pastoral ministry, but I had never actually been in a congregation who was served by a woman."

"Another hindrance would be putting ministry together with family priorities--how we put our call alongside our commitment to marriage and how you put those values over against each other. I still struggle with that one."

"I didn't have that many hindrances. And I don't know if I was too unaware to know them, but I don't think I was. You do need to remember that I was in my home territory. I was around northern Indiana and middle Indiana where people knew me and that may have been part of what cushioned any hindrance. I do not remember any hassle about being a woman preacher. The church has been good to me and ministry has been good to me. Let me say this. I think one thing that may have influenced this. I did not have in the 1940s and 1950s the baggage of this women's liberation thing. In more recent years, I think they hung that baggage on a lot of women that had a sincere call to ministry. My day and age was not colored by that."

"I was trying to think of those people who have been models for me. I wish I could think of some women, but I can't. That's really sad."

<u>Meaning of Ministry</u>

"I have a sharp distinction in my mind about parish ministry and all other forms of ministry. Ministry for me is something that can take place virtually anywhere and virtually anytime, by virtually anybody. It is that responsiveness to God's spirit in connection with other people. With the minister becoming the conduit of God's love. I could be effective in ministry working in a steel mill in terms of my relationships with comrades or in the classroom, or in most any setting. I see parish ministry, and the sole justification that I can think of for parish ministry, is to train people to do the work of ministry. And one of my frustrations has been that very few people within the church believe that . . .. We send our pastors off to get the training, then we bring them back to our congregations and put them to work doing things that other people could do and should be doing rather than having them involved in training us to do the work."

"In my youth I was a minister because God wanted me to be. I was serving God. I had at that time no interest in people. I detested people. I was pretty much of a loner. And I think my theology has changed a good bit in that respect. At first I served people and I worked with people because God told me I had to. I think now I see it as I work with people and serve people because I see that's where God is."

"I thought I could be a mother and a wife and be a pastor and do it all and do it all well. And I couldn't. I was very, very ill and spent seven months in bed. And I learned a lot about my ministry when

I was laying there not able to do anything. And I learned how to be ministered to. That was very important in my ministering then from then on. I grew a lot in not giving the nice little pat answers and that kind of thing."

"I had some kind of vague knowing or awareness that changes need to happen in the world. That the world needed leadership. That people needed leadership and that this was a major, significant challenge to the church. I can't be much more specific about that. It had more to do with influencing people and structures and concerns than it did with personal salvation. I felt if I was going to be in a career in leadership and work at change, then to work through the church was a natural thing to do."

"Our definition of ministry as something that belongs in the lap of the ordained is very hurtful to the denomination and to the church in general. Basically, what ministry means to me is to be in the service of Jesus Christ. We are called to be the embodiment of Christ in the world. How can we present the message of redemption, hope to a world that is filled with despair and misery? How can we serve the poor? How can we serve the sick and the imprisoned? How can we bring hope to the hopeless?"

"There is a tendency for pastors to become too reverent. To be set above rather than set-apart. Consequently, a lot of people in the church are in danger of losing their self concept of being ministers because they feel that is the pastor's role."

"After seven years in ministry I love it more now. I can't think of anything else I'd want to be. I could take a job in social work or professional counseling or something, but the things I think of that I'd like to be if I weren't in the pastorate are manual labor type things. Like a weaver or a mid-wife. That's the frustrating thing, but also the joy of ministry. Your work is never done. You're always involved with people. Things are always changing."

"Now when I think about the church and my role in it, I've really become convinced that what happened to me in my path to becoming a minister is what really ought to happen in some form or another to everybody who becomes a Christian. I guess it's the old 'priesthood of all believers' idea. I like to see my role in ministry as one who encourages people to figure what their gifts are, to see what it is that God has given them to do in life. The church should be that kind of place that encourages people to get about the business of doing ministry and then to come together to celebrate what God's been doing in their lives throughout the week in worship. Then to go out again and be in ministry."

<u>Role and Status of the Pastor</u>

"My desire was never to go into ministry or to work for the church. It sounded to me like something you married. I really was not interested in that."

"Part of what I struggled with for a long time is to see the pastorate as really a status position. I have seen families discourage their children from even thinking about the ministry. I've got the feeling in seeing some of the people who have gone into the ministry that maybe if you can't find your way in anything else, go into the ministry. I would like for children to think of the ministry as a high calling and as something that takes the very best people, not something that just is kind of catchall for leftovers and incompetents."

"I think maybe that the secret of ministry is to be available to people and to let them know you care, to let them know they are loved by their pastor. If they know that, they will hear you in the pulpit and they'll even overlook some of the shortcomings. And I guess having been brought up on a dairy farm where we worked from early morning to late at night, seven days a week, I've been a workaholic. In pastoral work I often worked seventy, eighty hours a week until I got old enough I couldn't work quite that many. I do not see how anybody can be pastor of a large church without putting in that kind of hours if he wants to minister to all the people."

"I guess a part of my resistance was my feeling that people so often tried to put the pastor on a pedestal. And I never felt like a pedestal was where I was supposed to be. I felt deeply that we were a church of a priesthood of all believers and no one really deserved a pedestal. And in my experience I have not experienced anyone who did not have feet of clay, including myself."

"I think one of the reasons I decided on pastoral ministry was that I saw in the way some pastoral ministers performed something I didn't really like. And I wanted to get into it to make a change. It had to do with being more people oriented and dealing with people in a more honest way rather than just teaching them."

"There is distinct imagery in some churches where the pastor is the head honcho. That there are times when the pastor is, kind of, the one to be served. I resist and rebel against that with all my being."

Finances

"Western Pennsylvania subscribed to a ministers Book of the Month Club. And I don't know who did the selecting at Elgin, but it was a tremendous selection of books. And they sent them to me free every month. As I got into seminary, there were loans offered at Elgin that were disappearing loans. And I remember when the first one expired, I got a little letter saying this is to let you know that your loan has been cancelled because of our five years of preaching. I wrote back and expressing how much I appreciated the fact that the money was available for me to go to seminary in the first place. He wrote to me then and said that was the first time anybody had written back thanking the brotherhood for the cancellation of the loan."

"I remember my son had quite a different experience. It was a little discouraging and disheartening. He got very minimum support from his home congregation in the licensing and ordination process. And absolutely no help financially. He finally pressed the congregation for a little help, but had to go back year after year and felt like he was begging instead of being supported."

"The hurdle is paying the loans back, not taking them out. When you're paying back three loans as a team, that is painful. I never had any anger at the call or at the education that I got. It was just the frustration of people not understanding. And I don't want the issues of finance to become issues in ministry. And that can be real difficult not to do."

"It is difficult to have people who are not used to evaluating personnel to try to do that because they don't know how to do it, they don't know the questions to ask. It took me a long time to realize that people don't always mean what they say. It doesn't always come out right. . . . It is a little difficult to have your salary right out there and have fifty or twenty people talking about it and each of them have different ideas. We have, I think, tried to live fairly plainly and I think that if you're going into the pastorate, you have to make that decision. You can't really drive around in BMWs or have a real fancy house, because people get confused with your being a spiritual leader and your being very materialistic. I think that that kind of goes with the territory."

"We didn't see how we would have money to go to Bethany, but my wife had been working and we did have a house of practically brand new furniture. So we had a public sale and sold our furniture so we would have money to go to seminary. That was an act of faith."

"I went from about $20,000 a year as a carpenter to less than $7,000 as a pastor. But I never regretted it."

Education

"In terms of getting started, nobody came and said anything to me about how you go about preparing sermons or writing sermon notes or anything like that. Our Elder in charge said after the election, 'You be prepared to bring the message in three weeks.' He was pretty abrupt. But you learn by doing. The congregation was very sympathetic and understanding and didn't have high expectations of Billy Graham or anything. I'm sure we had a lot of rough spots to get over, but it was basically learn by doing."

"I don't know what kind of pastor I would be or if I would still be in pastoral ministry if I had graduated from Claremont. Because I didn't really get a base there. I was just getting a lot of issues. So I think Bethany and its colloquium process was very important in deciding for pastoral ministry."

"For me colloquium and Bethany was a part of the formation. Another critical experience for me was Clinical Pastoral Education. I tore down a lot of barriers. If I wouldn't have had that experience, I don't think I would be nearly as effective in working with people. And that's part of my journey. So I need to name that. That was a painful part of my journey, but a very important part."

"Bob Mock was the minister to students at the time, and he encouraged me to not major in religion which I thought I was going to do, rather to major in secondary education but not to lose the ministry. He said sometimes people get into the ministry and discover ministry is not for them. And maybe it would be well if I had something I could fall back on. So with that encouragement I made a clear decision to get a bachelor of science degree in secondary education to teach biology."

From the Perspective of Congregational Leaders

In addition to the twenty-seven interviews with set-apart leaders, six congregational lay leaders (moderators, board chairs, ministry commission chairs) were interviewed. The following are quotations from these interviews:

"There have been a number of people going to Bethany from our congregation. For most of them I think it has been a personal decision. I don't think the church has done a lot of foster this. I feel that we could do more to give them a sense of calling from the local church."

"The program has been weak in the local church and I think school activities are a lot more demanding now than they were a generation ago. Particularly in the sports and music areas. So it is hard for a good youth program to take hold and dominate kid's lives in any significant way."

"I guess we want our kids to have complete freedom in their choice of careers and so on. We don't want to pressure them or brainwash them. We don't want to put feelings of guilt in their minds if they don't decide to do this. So we don't do the obvious simple encouragement. I know our son tells how an experience he had with his grandfather. His grandfather said, 'Grandson, you really ought to go into the ministry. You have the gift of gab.' And he laughs about that. But that made an influence on his life at that age. And we ought to do a little more of that, I think."

"I'll admit to a sense of loss, so to speak, when our son changed from law to ministry. Thinking all his life he's going to be living on a small income and giving up many things. I think I've gotten over that feeling, but it definitely was a real feeling for a while. Because we knew he had talents and we felt he would do well in whatever field he chose, and there's a certain prestige that goes with being a lawyer that isn't there with ministry."

"Speaking personally, I feel uncomfortable in encouraging people in terms of ministry. It means a sacrifice. It means being in a tough job. It means not having the kind of income that one could have in other areas and therefore I hold back. Across the 30 years of my involvement in East Chippewa we have licensed about 5 people and a couple of those were ordained. All of these persons came more out of a personal sense of challenge or commitment rather than encouragement on the part of the church. I generally feel the people of the church are concerned about ministry but don't quite know how to act on their concern."

"I feel like we're missing a lot of people that might be potentials. Because we're waiting for them to make the move."

"We expect pastors to be all things to all people. And really just expect too much in the way of demands on their time and on their abilities. We went through the search process looking for a new minister and everybody wants a great preacher, a super administrator, a caring family-type person, an excellent counsellor, involved in ecumenical activities and perfect in everything he does and get along well with the youth and the older people. And we expect them to work 14 hours a day, 7 days a week. So it's very difficult and then we expect them to do that without paying for it. And they've got a family they've got to support too."

"One of the areas, when you're looking at the future, is getting the kids when they are in high school. You talk to people who are ministers now--in their 50's and 60's--and almost all were called to go into the ministry when they were in high school. The congregation just said 'You are going to be a minister' and they did. And they've turned out to be very good ministers. And I know when I was in high school in the youth group here at LaVerne, nobody was saying anything like that. Going into ministry was never raised as an option of something you might want to do."

Concluding Observations

Gordon Hoffert, a 1989 Bethany graduate, says it well: "The call to ministry cannot be bottled or programmed. It always has both corporate and personal dimensions which are deeply imbedded in our faith pilgrimages."

These stories bear witness to these dimensions of the call to minstry. They are testimonies that illumine pilgrimages of faith and reach out to other pilgrims on the way.

CHAPTER FIVE

A THEOLOGY OF MINISTRY FOR THE CHURCH OF THE BRETHREN

Melanie A. May

Since its beginnings, the Church of the Brethren has recognized ministry as a basic expression of the church's life. Indeed, Brethren have affirmed that ministry is the work of the whole church. Remembering that we who are baptized into Christ's living Body, the church, are "a chosen people, a royal priesthood, a holy nation . . . " (I Peter 2:9), we view the church as the "priesthood of all believers".[1]

But our sense of what the "priesthood of all believers" means is no longer substantive or strong. Although we still speak of all our baptized members, laity and ordained alike, as belonging to the "priesthood of all believers," the Church of the Brethren, like many mainline Protestant churches in the United States, is experiencing a leadership crisis. As membership in our churches has steadily declined, so has the quantity and quality of candidates for ordained ministry.[2]

The decline of ministerial candidates is not only a current concern for the Church of the Brethren. At the 1953 Annual Conference meeting in Colorado Springs, "concern for ministerial recruitment" was raised and the "present critical shortage of ministers" was put before the delegates.[3] In 1958, a query considering an "urgent" need for a "Guidance Program for Licensed Ministers" was brought to Annual Conference. A committee was appointed and a report came to Annual Conference in 1959:

> The committee interprets the basic intent of the query to be the necessity of conserving men and women for the ministry. Many individuals are lost to the ministry because they have never been called. Other persons are

> lost to the ministry after they have been called, because of many factors. We consider it to be within the scope of this paper to suggest reasons for these losses and to make recommendations for the conservation of men and women for the ministry of the church.[4]

In response, a "Special Resolution on Ministerial Recruitment" requested that the General Brotherhood Board "undertake an intensive research study of the recruitment and conservation of the ministry, with particular reference to attractions and deterrents of the ministry and the causes of pastoral withdrawal".[5]

It is significant that, at least since 1951, all Annual Conference statements on the ministry are focused on the licensed and ordained ministry. There is no substantive address of the "priesthood of all believers." This suggests that a preoccupation with set-apart (and largely salaried) ministry has not nurtured our foundational sense that ministry belongs to the whole church. Corresponding with this lack of clarity about just what we mean by the ministry of all, our understanding and practice of calling has been diminished. Congregations, communities of the "priesthood of all believers," rarely act as groups called to form and mentor members into ministers, and then to discern and call everyone into service.

The 1985 Annual Conference statement on ministry opens a way to strengthen our foundational sense of ministry for the sake of the future. This statement grounds understandings of calling and ordination in our understanding of the church, thus reaffirming that ministry fundamentally belongs to the whole people of God. To paraphrase Yves Congars: "At bottom there can be only one sound and sufficient theology of [ministry], and that is a 'total ecclesiology'".[6]

THE CHURCH

"The Church," says Congars, "is an organic body:"

> On the one hand, each member, each cell of this body is living; on the other, all the members do not have the same function in the body, and so its one single soul, the Spirit of Christ, does not animate all the members for the same purpose and in the same way. . . . But all, complete with their differences, form one single "subject," one single responsible person, that is the Ecclesia, the Church. [7]

This understanding resonates with our own understanding of the Church, which is clearly and well stated in the 1985 Annual Conference Minutes:

> The church understands itself as the people of God, the body of Christ, and the fellowship of the Holy Spirit. As the people of God, the church is rooted in the purposes of God as the Creator and Lord of all history. As the body of Christ, the church looks to Jesus Christ as the source and norm of its life and as the definitive expression of God's purposes for all life. As the fellowship of the Holy Spirit, the church experiences God's presence in power to lead the church into the future, to equip it for its mission, and to evoke praise of the One who has called it into being. The church is both a people of God and a people of a history, a divine community and a human community. . . . The church is one. . . . The church is both called out of the world and sent into the world. God's people are to be holy as God is holy, committed to a special identity and calling. To be called out or set apart, however, does not mean cut off, whether geographically or socially. The church lives in an interdependent relationship with many other human communities, political and financial, secular and religious, national and international. Moreover, the world in which

the church lives remains the object of God's love. It is the world, therefore, which is the arena of the church's mission.

The church's mission is to create new communities of faith and life which embody God's shalom and through which Christ works to bring renewal to both persons and society. Such an understanding of mission is deeply rooted in our Pietist/Anabaptist heritage, and it differs both from the understanding of those who limit mission to the evangelization of individuals and from the understanding of others who limit mission to the secular transformation of corporate structures. The church is a sign and instrument of God's kingdom but is not itself identical with the kingdom. Christ calls us to participate in the coming of God's reign, embodying that reign in our life together and witnessing to that reign in our life in the world. The new creation which is the final goal of God's reign, however, is broader than the church and must not be equated with any particular ecclesiastical structures. Such a reminder is necessary to guard us from succumbing to institutional self-preservation as an end in itself or to a self-righteous approach to our mission in the world.

The church as a community of saints exists in the form of congregations bound to particular places, but it also has a global identity which is fuller than (and sometimes challenges) the identity of any local community. It exists here and now but also reaches out across all ages. It is earthly and transcendent, visible and invisible. The articulation of the church's mission must be attentive to all of these dimensions of its character.[8]

Throughout the centuries of the Christian tradition there has been a tension about how to live as Christians in the world. This tension is sometimes characterized by what are called "church" and "sect" ways. The "church" way is identified as closely aligned with the social power-holders in nation and state. The "sect" way is identified as peripheral to established authorities, often standing apart from or even over against them. Christians and churches all experience tension between the ideals akin to the intimate, sectarian Jesus movement and the hard realities of the world where we easily compromise our values (in the hope to maintain our organization's life). Both "churchly, institutional" and "sectarian, intimate" motifs and needs are manifest in the believing community's life. Accordingly, ministerial leadership must be able to recognize each and to discern in which specific situations and with what particular people each emphasis is needed. [9]

Brethren have tended to associate intimate community with living as a family, looking to familial intimacy as the backbone of the continuity of the church and its ministry. Our near identification of intimacy with church now contributes to loosening our bonds to church as the bonds of family intimacy are loosening around us and among us. Yet this loosening offers an occasion for us to join in knitting more diverse and inclusive bonds in years to come: bonds based on a clear distinction between intimate community and ekklesia.

Ekklesia is not family. Ekklesia is the new creation in Christ, God's household, the church. Unlike intimate communities, God's household is not difficult for outsiders to enter. And, as scripture richly attests, God's household is a place where leaders and those in authority (are) change(d). Intimate communities find identity in past experiences and are nourished by familiar repetition. But for its life as God's witness in the world, the church needs something more accessible and future-oriented than intimacy alone can offer. From its beginning, the church visible in the New Testament included both the elements of institutional organization and the warmth of the intimate community. Both together provide the church's continuity and vitality. [10]

THE CALL

Several Annual Conferences since 1950 have spoken about the call to ministry. The 1951 Annual Conference stated:

> Men and women before entering the ministry of the church should feel the call of God to serve. God's call may come in such ways as (a) To the individual, who, having heard the call, may volunteer to elder, pastor, or pastoral board; (b) Through the church, which may lay it upon the heart of the person to accept and serve after prayer and under guidance of the Holy Spirit. [11]

The 1975 Annual Conference confirmed:

> Within the Church of the Brethren, ordination originates in the following ways: (1) The ordinand may receive the "call" to serve from God, through the ministry of the Holy Spirit in his or her life (Mark 3:14; John 15:16; Acts 10:42; Gal. 1:15; I Tim. 2:7). The ordinand makes known the "call" to the local church for counsel and eventual recommendation to the district. (2) The ordinand may be called by the church, through the local congregation, the "call" being confirmed and consummated by the district. This procedure assumes that the ordinand feels the "call" is from God through the church (Acts 1:21-26; 14:23). Such a "call" may be initiated by a pastor, a local church or district ministry commission, by the vote of a church in council (as was usual in early Church of the Brethren tradition) or by other church bodies or whose leadership.[12]

The fullest statement about calling is found in the minutes of the 1985 Annual Conference:

> In the Old Testament, the people of God were frequently described as a qahal, a word whose meaning

derives from the word for voice (qol). So Israel understood itself as the people called out by God's voice from amongst other peoples as servants of God's purpose. A key New Testament word for call is klesis, taken from ekklesia, one of the words we translate as church. When understood in this way, church, or ekklesia, refers to the ones "called out," like those who are summoned by a herald to become part of a special assembly or gathering. So, call, or klesis, in its foundational New Testament usage, is the call to discipleship, the call to follow after Jesus (Nachfolge), the call to the ministry of all believers. Its first and most general expression is baptism by which we become members in Christ's crucified-risen body, the newly constituted people of God or corporate humanity. This call not only precedes but also empowers our response, for it is based on the objective work of salvation accomplished in Jesus Christ.

Occasionally, in the New Testament, klesis is used as the personal, individual call to particular services. Examples are Romans 1:1 and I Corinthians 1:1 in which Paul refers to himself as having been called to the work of an apostle. But, even there, the thought is both objective and corporate and presupposes an understanding of the way the "Body of Christ" differentiates into its parts, with each part being essential for the well being and the effective functioning of the total organism. From such references we are assured that there is New Testament warrant for speaking of call in a personal, individual sense, as when we currently feature one's call to a particular form of the set-apart ministry. It is important, though, to keep before us the wider range of scriptural meanings.

The call to set-apart ministry is of God. It is mediated through persons who represent the community of faith. It is deeply personal, but it is not a private affair. It is both a profound inner conviction and the testing of the conviction by the church. It is, therefore, both the call of God and the call of the church.[13]

But our understanding of the call, like our understanding of ministry, features the set-apart ministry and the internal affairs of the church. If churches of the magisterial reformation have let go the radicality of the declaration of the priesthood of all believers, we have let go Luther's sense of Christian vocation in the world as in the church. Luther's understanding of vocation was formed in response to the medieval Roman sharp division between monks, nuns, and priests who had callings and Christians in the so-called secular world who had no vocations. Luther extended vocation to include all stations in life, clerical and lay. Luther's concept of vocation is also applicable to both of the two kingdoms, the kingdom of creation and the kingdom of grace, Luther distinguishes. In both kingdoms, believers gladly serve others in whatever situation.

Calvin agreed with Luther that all Christians have vocations in the world that are far more than their occupations. But, in contrast to Luther's affirmation that God gives a Christian a vocation in the world is to encourage a life of loving service, Calvin believed God gave a Christian a vocation for the proper ordering of human life, lest everything be thrown into chaos. And while Luther saw a vocation as a means whereby God bestowed gifts upon all humankind, Calvin celebrated a vocation as a means of giving glory to God.

As Anabaptists we dissent from the blessing of the sociocultural, economic, and political status quo that accompanies Luther's and Calvin's understandings of vocation. We may nevertheless learn from them about the radicality of Christ's reign in the world. For God's calling lays claim to life, to a person's whole life, both in the community of faith and in the world.

All members of the household of God together constitute "a royal priesthood." The confession of the priesthood of all believers is based on five scriptural passages (I Peter 2:4-5; 2:9-10; Revelation 1:5-6; 5:9-10; 20:6); all five passages refer to the priesthood of all believers in a corporate rather than in an individual sense. Each believer can exercise a priestly function in relation to her or his sisters and brothers, and believers together as the body of Christ can exercise a priestly function in relation to the world. As William Beahm put it: " . . . the work of the ministry is so wide and so urgent that it will take a whole kingdom of priests to fulfill it".[14]

SET-APART MINISTRY

According to the Acts of the Apostles, the early church designated seven members to assume special responsibility for the distribution of food to the believers. The Twelve said: "Pick out from among you seven men of good repute, full of the Spirit and of wisdom, whom we may appoint to this duty." We read that after the selection "these they set before the apostles, and they prayed and laid their hands upon them" (Acts 6:1-6). Later in Acts we read that in Antioch "while [the believers] were worshipping the Lord and fasting, the Holy Spirit said, 'Set apart for me, Barnabas and Saul for the work to which I have called them.' So after they had fasted and prayed, they placed their hands on them and sent them off" (Acts 13:2-3). Saul, "who was also called Paul," and Barnabas ordained elders of the churches at Lystra, Iconium, and Antioch for the purpose of serving as pastors (Acts 14:23). At Ephesus, Paul called the elders of the church and instructed them: "Keep watch over yourselves and all the flock of which the Holy Spirit has made you overseers" (Acts 20:28).

The Church of the Brethren has understood that some members are "set apart" for particular ministries. In Schwarzenau, seven cast lots to see who would baptize Alexander Mack, whom the others set apart to baptize them. Our congregations have nurtured various forms of set apart ministerial leadership: from the free ministry and the salaried ministry to Education for a Shared Ministry and Training in Ministry ministerial models.

The 1985 Annual Conference Minutes state:

> The church needs leaders, persons ordained or set-apart by their ministry, to remind us that our life, as theirs, comes from God. Yet we know, as Israel learned under the kingship, that even a God-initiated office tempts the people and office-holder alike to behave as if the one holding office were "over" those among whom he or she holds leadership. Jesus' death, relinquishing control "over" even those he came to save, defies that interpretation of ordination. But subject to misinterpretation as ordination is, the people of God do need such leaders as set-apart ministers who are able to serve God and God's people so that the whole church ministers as Christ's living presence to and for all creation. As God became human in Jesus Christ, thus voluntarily becoming vulnerable to our misunderstandings, so God becomes human in the lives of persons today, remaining vulnerable to human perception and passion, yet appropriating such "treasures in earthen vessels to show that the transcendent power belongs to God and not to us" (2 Cor. 4:7b).[15]

The Annual Conference goes on to clarify that, although we Brethren have often spoken about set-apart ministry in functional terms, there has also been "a persistent effort to hold together what a person does and what a person symbolizes, or represents, in reference to ministry".[16]

In this regard, it is important to recall that the New Testament understanding of ministry is more diverse than the understandings of our day. The General Board, in a report to the 1969 Annual Conference, stated:

One of the New Testament terms for "minister" is diakonos (from which our term deacon is a transliteration). It means, literally, a servant. Anyone who sincerely follows Christ is his diakonos (John 12:26). Jesus defined greatness in terms of being a minister or servant (Matthew 2:26).

Nowhere in the New Testament is the word <u>hierus</u>, "priest," employed as the equivalent of the set-apart ministry as we know it today. In the words of 1 Peter 2:9, as God's people the entire Christian community is "a royal priesthood".[17]

The call to the set-apart ministry "is not derived from God's call to the whole people of God and neither does this call to distinctive responsibilities have precedence over the general call to all members of the body of Christ".[18] Both calls come from God; each is a gift and a naming of gifts as discerned and designated by the church. Samuel J. Mikolaski, citing Bernard Cooke, is bolder as he comments:

> There has been a failure to understand the relationship between ordained ministry and the ministry of the Christian community as a whole. Euphemisms such as "the priesthood of all believers" and "the apostolate of the laity" mislead because the corporate ministry of the church is "a commission that pertains to all baptized Christians including those designated for specialized ministries." Hence, the ministerial function of clergy is to "sustain and nurture the corporate ministry of the church."[19]

If we take the ministry of all baptized believers seriously, ". . . this will mean a Copernican change for many of us: all the members of the church have received grace and are therefore called to service or--to say exactly the same thing--called to ministry. This ministry of the

> church is entrusted to the 'saints,' to such ordinary people as are most members of the church".[20]

FOR ALL THE SAINTS

The early second-century distinction between klerikos and laikos, that is, between clergy and laity, was a distinction of function, which was without a difference in status. It was a distinction of function "not in an official civic sense, but in an ecclesial sense:

> " . . . it is the liturgical and sacramental expression of the sense of community that what happens in the ecclesia is a gift of God's Spirit and not an expression of the autonomy of the church. . . . The tension between an ontological-sacerdotalist view of the ministry on one hand and a purely functionalist view on the other must . . . be resolved by a theological view of the church's ministry as a charismatic office, the service of leading the community, and therefore as an ecclesial function within the community and accepted by the community. Precisely in this way it is a gift of God.[21]

The resolution resides in the committed community. In committed community, ministerial functions are inextricably interwoven with personal presence as reflection and practice.

Quakers have also wrestled with the early church concepts of klerikos and laikos; indeed, they have rejected the distinction between clergy and laity. The fundamental basis of their rejection of this distinction was the effort to be faithful to the New Testament portrait of ministry. From their beginning, Quakers could discern in first-century Christianity no counterpart to what their world meant by clergy or laity. This is to say, Quakers were not merely anticlerical:

> The idea of the lay Christian is, indeed, as objectionable as is the idea of the clerical Christian. For this reason the Quaker

> must always fight on two fronts simultaneously. To use a Biblical analogy, [the Quaker] must "beware of the leaven of the Pharisees and the leaven of Herod" (Mark 8: 15). It is wrong to be a [layperson], if by [layperson] is meant, as it popularly is, a person who is primarily a supporter of the work which the clergy do, rather than a vital member of the Christian team. In contemporary parlance, because of its use in connection with the law and with medicine, the word [layperson] means a person who does not or cannot practice. It ought to be obvious to all that there is no rightful place in the Christian cause for anyone whose function can be so described. For this reason, the practical Quaker purpose is sometimes described as that of "the abolition of the laity." There is, in any case, no justification for the role of the mere observer. Christianity, when it truly understands itself, can never be a spectator sport.[22]

The very dichotomy, along with the concepts of clergy and laity, is thus denied.

"Saints" are integral to leadership in congregations. "Saints" are "the consolers, confidants, and care-givers who have come to symbolize what it means to belong in that particular congregation."[23] Together with the organizers and the traditional leaders, e.g., the storytellers and the community "mothers," the "saints" are the leadership of the local church.

While this rich biblical image, the "saints," may be helpful for re-vitalizing our understanding of the ministry of all baptized believers, we need a more fundamental transformation of our minds. The whole people of God will hear a call to ministry, that is, only as we can confess "we are the church." Many members feel that the church is somebody else, whether ordained ministers or professional church administrators or a few persons in the local church power structure. It is paramount for members to feel and affirm that together we constitute the living Body of Christ in the world.

This then points to another dimension of this transformation of our minds. Members must confess "we are the church;" we must also be clear that we are representatives of Christ in the world. In our day, the split between the church as religious and the world as secular subverts our self-understanding as members of Christ's body. Many members think that they spent a relatively small part of their time engaged in ministry, assuming that the time they spent working in the world is devoted to secular rather than religious duties. As we extend our understanding of calling to encompass vocation in the world, the sense of the ministry of all members may be enhanced, for it will be clear that neither the functional nor the representative aspects of ministry adhere only to those set-apart.

Indeed, the understanding of calling as encompassing vocation in the world is grounded in an understanding of the church. The church has a mission beyond its own boundaries; the church is "driven by the terms of [its] own worship [of God, who has created the world and called it good] to reach out in concern beyond [its] borders."[24] This mission is first of all not anything the church does, but what the church is: the light of the world, the salt of the earth, a city set on a hill.

Another obstacle to this sense of the ministry of all members is the present predisposition to regard ordained ministers as the experts or the professionals. On one hand, many church leaders have bought into an "adulterated careerist image of a 'professional' in which theology and redemption are secondary and sacrificed to practical know-how and therapeutic-managerial ideals." [25] On the other hand, the professional is one who masters a body of knowledge and uses it in a disciplined way, not for self-advancement but for the valued end that is "professed." This ideal of the professional could at once help pastors climb down from their pedestals to take their place along with other professional callings and help the practice of ministry be informed by considered assessments of the human situation more than by a mere exercise of skills.

The challenge to the church in this era of professionalization and secularization is to re-vitalize our understanding of ministry in relation to the life of the church and the world. A key concept for this re-vitalization is servanthood. Jesus' ministry was servant ministry: "I am among you as one who serves" (Luke 22:27). The figure of the Good Samaritan is a foremost model of the characteristic ministry of Jesus:

> When we ponder the love which [God] has made known in [Jesus Christ], we suddenly realize that the Jericho road, the world of [human] need, is Christ's own place.[26]

The figure of Jesus kneeling down to wash his disciples' feet, the one who "did not count equality with God a thing to be grasped" (Phil. 2: 6), is also a model for ministry in Christ's way. In our era of the expert and professionalism in ministry, the image of the Suffering Servant and, accordingly, of the minister as servant is a model of mutuality for the empowered and empowering partnership of clergy and laity.[27]

A second key concept is the ministry of reconciliation:

> A Christian is a person seeking to lead a life in conformity with the life of Jesus Christ, and with the vitality that was manifested in that life. Therefore every Christian life is a priestly life. . . . And not only of his life: we become sharers in all the richness of his diakonia, his proclamation, and his deed of sanctification. In other words, the Christian is responsible for the mission of the whole church. . . . For a Christian a profession is more than just a way of earning one's daily bread. It is a way of actualizing service, concord, and reconciliation among human beings. It is a means of bringing human beings nearer one another, in the transcendence of divisions, and in humble, hushed acceptance of anguishing and inescapable situations.

> The diakonia of reconciliation is to be exercised by all Christians. This makes them priests, men as well as women, for they are all to prolong in time and space the unifying function of Christ, the eternal High Priest.[28]

These concepts of servanthood and reconciliation strike deep cords in Church of the Brethren hearts. Our present context of crisis calls us to another aspect of this practice of ministry: the task of proclamation of the Gospel in and for the world. While our service has been in and for the world, we Brethren have not readily spoken about our faith as a witness to the world nor often dared prophetic pronouncement. We have not always recognized that the call to service and to the ministry of reconciliation finally depends on our willingness to respond to the call "out from the inner life of the church into the highways and hedges, out into the areas of sore tension and need, to apply there the healing of God's righteous and redeeming love".[29] In this sense, "but not because of an unbroken line of formal leaders," the church is apostolic:

> [The church] is apostolic because, like the early apostles, [the church] is set in the world with an apostolic mission. [The church] is the light of the world and the salt of the earth. [The church] is a city set upon a hill which cannot be hid. [The church] is the Body of Christ, set to fulfill [Christ's] mission of reconciliation and peace.[30]

And, in all things, we are all called to give glory to God as we work for our neighbors' good, recognizing that ultimately the vocation of the whole creation is praise to God.

NOTES

Introduction

1. Peter Steinfels, "Shortage of Qualified New Clergy Causing Alarm for U.S. Religions," The New York Times, Sunday, July 9, 1989.

2. Ibid.

3. Ibid.

4. See Dean Hoge, Future of Catholic Leadership: Responses to the Priest Shortage (Kansas City: Sheed and Ward, 1987). See also James R. Kelly, "Data and Mystery: A Decade of Studies on Catholic Leadership," America, November 18, 1989, pp. 345-350, for a survey of research funded by the Lilly Endowment.

5. See Richard A. Schoenherr and Annemette Sorensen, "Decline and Change in the U.S. Catholic Church," Report #5, CROS (Madison, WI: University of Wisconsin, 1981). See also Laurie Felknor, ed., The Crisis in Religious Vocations: An Inside View (New York and Mahwah: Paulist Press, 1989).

6. See Thomas P. Rausch, "Forming Priests for Tomorrow's Church: The Coming Synod," America, February 24, 1990, pp. 168-172, for a preview of the synod discussion.

7. See, for example, "The Study of Ministry in the Evangelical Lutheran Church in America: Report to the 1989 Churchwide Assembly." Division for Ministry Report, Reports and Records, Volume 1 and 2, 1989 ELCA Churchwide Assembly. Reprinted 10/89.

8. Wade Clark Roof and William McKinney, American Mainline Religion: Its Changing Shape and Future (New Brunswick and London: Rutgers University Press, 1987), p. 6.

9. See Robert Wuthnow, The Struggle for America's Soul: Evangelicals, Liberals, and Secularism (Grand Rapids: William B. Eerdmans, 1989).

10. Steinfels, "Shortage of Qualified New Clergy Causing Alarm for U.S. Religions."

11. Zikmund's book-length work is still in preparation. This quotation was cited in a preview of her work by Linda-Marie Delloff in "New Roles, New Power for Women in the Church, Progressions: A Lilly Endowment Occasional Report, vol. 2, issue 1 (January 1990), p. 15.

12. Ibid.

13. See Lynn N. Rhodes, Co-Creating: A Feminist Vision of Ministry (Philadelphia: The Westminster Press, 1987) for a discussion of the newly creative perspectives and practices of women in ministry.

14. Leonard I. Sweet, "The Ladder or Cross: The Plover Report," p. 5.

15. Roger Finke and Rodney Stark, "How the Upstart Sects Won America: 1776-1850," Journal for the Scientific Study of Religion, 1989, 28 (1): 38.

16. See Dean R. Hoge, Jackson Carroll, and Francis K. Sheets, Patterns of Parish Leadership: Cost and Effectiveness in Four Denominations (Kansas City: Sheed & Ward, 1989), pp. 89ff.

17. See Brethren Life and Thought, vol. VI, no. 3 (Summer 1961) and vol. IX, no. 4 (Autumn 1964) for papers from theological study conferences in 1960 and 1964, conferences at which Church of the Brethren, free church, pietist, and anabaptist understandings of the church were discussed.

18. See "Leadership Needs and Ministry Issues," Minutes of the 199th Recorded Annual Conference of the Church of the Brethren, p. 138-156.

19. See Pamela Brubaker, She Hath Done What She Could (Elgin: Brethren Press, 1985), p. 136. See also pp. 135-150 on women and the set-apart ministry.

20. Ibid., p. 140.

21. Ibid., p. 141.

22. Ibid., p. 146. See Brethren Life and Thought, vol. XXX, no. 1 (Winter 1985), guest edited by Nadine Pence Frantz and Lauree Hersch Meyer, for writings of Church of the Brethren women in ministry in contemporary contexts.

23. Robert E. Faus, "The Ministry Transition Project," p. 3. Unpublished report of sabbatical research, February-April, 1990.

24. Ibid., pp. 3-4.

25. Ibid., p. 4.

26. See David B. Eller, ed. Servants of the Word (Elgin: Brethren Press, 1990), a collection of the papers presented at this conference. See also John Howard Yoder, The Fullness of Christ: Paul's Revolutionary Vision of Universal Ministry (Elgin: Brethren Press, 1987), a study first published in 1969 and republished in preparation for the Eighth Believers' Church Conference at the initiative of the planning committee.

27. Among Rosemary Haughton's many books are these that are particularly relevant to a spirituality of ministry: The Transformation of Man: A Study of Conversion and Community (Springfield, IL.: Templegate, 1967); The Drama of Salvation (New York: The Seabury Press, 1975); The Passionate God (New York and Ramsey: Paulist Press, 1981); The Re-Creation of Eve (Springfield, IL.: Templegate Publishers, 1985).

Chapter One

1. Craig Dykstra, Vice President of the Lilly Endowment for the Regligion Section, is one among the mature "mainline" Christian scholars to insist practice, including the practice of ministry, is "what a community does." Dykstra means to emphasize the communal rather than individual nature of practice, and to highlight the significance of doing rather than developing theories about what concerns us, in this case, ministry.

2. See "A Theology of Ministry for the Church of the Brethren" Chapter Five in this book. See also Merle D. Strege, ed. Baptism and Church; A Believers' Church Vision, (Sagamore Books: Grand Rapids, 1986), which contains addresses and reflections from a Believers' Church Conference on baptism, the seventh in a series of "Continuing Conversations" among churches of the radical reformation tradition. See also David B. Eller, ed. Servants of the Word (Elgin: Brethren Press, 1990), which contains the papers from the eigth Believers' Church Conference. This conference considered Believers' Church perspectives on ministry together with the ministry section of the World Council of Churches' Baptism, Eucharist and Ministry text.

3. See John Cassel's interviews with some of the Church of the Brethren's most able ministers, "In Their Own Words," to sense how significant yet unpredictable, and even "accidental," the church's call to ministry is experienced to be.

4. See Robert Faus' survey, "Calling to Ministry in the Church of the Brethren," Chapter Three in this book. A particularly notable change in congregational presuppositions about the "call" was that the word is now used predominantly in reference to securing pastoral leadership. This is a significant change from earlier understandings of "call" as naming and claiming the gifts of members of Christ's body for the whole church's daily, set-apart, as well as pastoral ministries.

   Over the years, the Church of the Brethren has consistently concerned itself with matters of ministry, as witnessed by many post-World War II Annual Conference statements on the matter: 1951, "Advancement and Standards in the Ministry;" 1953, "Concern for Ministerial Recruitment;" 1953, "Functions of an Elder;" 1955, an unnamed report addressing biblical and historical background, local church moderator, moderator-pastor relationship, district elders' and moderators' council; 1957, another unnamed report addressing the licensed and ordained ministry, the ordained eldership, and the district elders, pastors, and moderators' council, as well as the district elders' council; 1957, "Ministerial Recruitment and Conservation"; 1959, "Guidance Program for Licensed Ministers; 1962, a list of "attractions and deterrents to the ministry and the causes of pastor withdrawal" in response to a "Special Resolution on Ministerial Recruitment;" 1969, "Ministerial Nomenclature;" 1970, "Recruitment and Training of Ministers From Minority Groups;" 1975, "The Ministry: Ordination and Family Life;" 1976, "Discipleship and Reconciliation;" 1977, "Marriage and Divorce: Special Problems for Leadership;" 1977, "The Layspeaker;" 1981, "Crisis in Transition Fund;" 1985, "Leadership Needs and Ministry Issues," 1986, "Licensed and Ordained Ministry;" and a 1987 General Board paper on "Ethics in Ministry Relations."

5. See, for example, Katie Funk Wiebe, "Can the Church Survive the Professionalization of its Leadership?" Gospel Herald (July 4, 1989): 482-83. Her concern for "professionalization" addresses the source and center of the church's values in hiring leaders, not the (needed) data and skills a skilled, trained leader is expected to engage in the service of the church.

6. Allen Bloom, The Closing of the American Mind (New York: Simon and Schuster, 1987), p. 341.

7. See Martin R. Saarinen, The Life Cycle of a Congregation (Washington D.C.: An Alban Institute Publication, 1986). His analysis relates the presence, strength, and balance of congregational energy, program,

administration, and inclusion to its "age" (and viability) as an ecclesial institution.

8. In an article in The Christian Century, "Revisioning Seminary as Ministry-Centered", Glenda Hope argues that we must "let go of the comforts of the private intellectual and therapeutic approaches to seminary education and move toward the terrors of public communal discipleship" (The Christian Century [February 1-8, 1989]), p. 110. William H. Willimon, Stanley Hauerwas, and Rebecca S. Chopp responded to Hope's article. As a whole, the discussion presses for more care in identifying for what formal ministry education is essential as well as useful, while insisting that the ordained ministry is but one of the church's ministries.

9. Gaylord Noyce, "The Pastor is (Also) a Professional," The Christian Century (November 2, 1988): 975-76.

10. Anne Wilson Schaef, Co-Dependence: Misunderstood - Mistreated (San Francisco: Harper & Row, 1986); Melody Beattie, Codependent No More (San Francisco: Harper & Row, 1987); Melody Beattie, Beyond Codependency and Getting Better All the time (San Francisco: Harper & Row, 1989).

11. See Leonard J. Sweet, "The Ladder or the Cross: The Plover Report" unpublished manuscript.

12. See Ann Douglas, Feminization of American Religion (New York: Alfred A. Knopf, 1977).

13. See E.D. Hirsch, Jr., Cultural Literacy: What Every American Needs to Know (Houghton Mifflin Co., 1987).

14. See Rick Simonson and Scott Walker, eds., The Graywolf Annual Five: Multicultural Literacy (Graywolf Press, 1988).

15. Note the study referred to in note 1.

16. See Rosemary Haughton, The Transformation of Man: A Study of Conversion and Community (Springfield, Illinois: Templegate, 1967) for an insightful discussion of these distinctive emphases.

17. A major conversation about the church's role and relevance in contemporary society is taking place. Sometimes sociological, sometimes ecclesial, sometimes economic and political, this conversation was searched

by Wade Clark Roof and William McKinney's in American Mainline Religion: Its Changing Shape and Future (New Brunswick and London: Rutgers University Press, 1987). See also David Heim's response, "Looking for the Mainline with Roof and McKinney," The Christian Century (June 1, 1988): 544-48, and Leonard I. Sweet, "From Catacomb to Basilica: The Dilemma of Oldline Protestantism," The Christian Century (November 2, 1988): 981-84. See also Stanley Hauerwas and William H. Willamon, Resident Aliens: Life in the Christian Colony (Nashville: Abingdon Press, 1989).

18. Terms for this present day discussion were mostly set by Max Weber The Sociology of Religion, trans. from German by Ephraim Fischoff, (Boston: Beacon Press, 1964). Originally published in 1922.

Chapter Two

1. Julia Esquivel, "I Am Not Afraid of Death," in Threatened with Resurrection: Poems and Prayers from an Exiled Guatemalan (Elgin, IL: The Brethren Press, 1982), p.65.

2. Revised Standard Version of Lukan reading.

3. See Julian of Norwich, Revelation of Divine Love, trans. by Clifton Wolters. (Harmondsworth, Middlesex, England: Penguin Books Ltd.) 1966.

Chapter Five

1. Alexander Mack, A Short and Plain View of the Outward Yet Sacred Rites and Ordinances of the House of God, 1799/1975, pp. 26-27. See also William M. Beahm, Studies in Christian Belief (Elgin: The Brethren Press, 1958), p. 241.

2. Roof and McKinney, American Mainline Religion: Its Changing Shape and Future (New Brunswick: Rutgers University Press, 1987).

3. Minutes of the Annual Conferences of the Church of the Brethren 1945-1954, compiled and edited by Ora W. Garber (Elgin: Brethren Publishing House, 1956), p. 192.

4. Minutes of the Annual Conferences of the Church of the Brethren 1955-1964, compiled and edited by Ora W. Garber (Elgin: The Brethren Press, 1965), p. 120.

5. Ibid., p. 255.

6. Yves Congars, Lay People in the Church: A Study for a Theology of Laity, rev. ed., trans. Donald Attwater (Westminister, MD.: The Newman Press, 1965), p. xvi.

7. Yves Congars, Laity, Church and World, trans. Donald Attwater (Baltimore: Helicon Press, 1960), p. 70.

8. Minutes of the 199th Recorded Annual Conference of the Church of the Brethren, pp. 117-118.

9. Carl Dudley and Earl Hilgert, New Testament Tensions and the Contemporary Church (Philadelphia: Fortress Press, 1987), pp. 32, 43.

10. Ibid., p. 34.

11. Minutes of the Annual Conferences of the Church of the Brethren 1945-1954, p. 128.

12. Minutes of the Annual Conference of the Church of the Brethren 1975-1979, compiled by Phyllis Kingery Ruff (Elgin: The Brethren Press, 1980), p. 63.

13. Minutes of the 199th Recorded Annual Conference of the Church of the Brethren, pp. 119-120.

14. Beahm, Studies in Christian Belief, p. 241.

15. Ibid., p. 120.

16. Ibid., p. 121.

17. Minutes of the Annual Conference of the Church of the Brethren 1965-1970, compiled and edited by William R. Eberly (Elgin: The Brethren Press, 1970), p. 410.

18. Donald R. Heiges, The Christian's Calling (Philadelphia: Fortress Press, 1984), p. 87.

19. "Universal Ministry in the Global Village," unpublished manuscript, p. 10. Cf. Bernard Cooke, Ministry of Word and Sacraments.

20. Hans-Ruedi Weber, Living in the Image of Christ: The Laity in Ministry (Geneva: World Council of Churches, 1986), pp. 71-72.

21. Edward C. Schillebeeck, Ministry: Leadership in the Community of Jesus Christ (New York: The Crossroads Publishing Co., 1985), pp. 68, 70.

22. D. Elton Trueblood, The People Called Quakers (New York: Harper & Row, Publishers, 1966), p. 115.

23. See Dudley and Hilgert, New Testament Tensions and the Contemporary Church, p. 73.

24. Beahm, Studies in Christian Belief, p. 244.

25. Leonard I. Sweet, "The Ladder or the Cross: The Plover Report," pp. 5-6.

26. Ronald E. Osborn, In Christ's Place: Christian Ministry in Today's World (St. Louis: The Bethany Press, 1967), p. 22.

27. See Robert Greenleaf, Servant Leadership: A Journey into the Nature of Legitimate Power and Greatness (New York: Paulist Press, 1977) and Lewis Mudge, In His Service: The Servant Lord and His Servant People (Philadelphia: The Westminster Press, 1959).

28. Leonardo Boff, Ecclesiogenesis: The Base Communities Reinvent the Church Maryknoll (Maryknoll: Orbis Books, 1986), pp. 91-92.

29. Beahm, Studies in Christian Belief, pp. 249-250.

30. Ibid., p. 250.

BIBLIOGRAPHY

The Context

Barbara Ehrenreich. Fear of Falling: The Inner Life of the Middle Class. New York: Pantheon Books, 1989.

This book explores the inner life of America's middle class, the class of most members of the Church of the Brethren and other oldline Protestant churches, elaborating the enormous power the vision and values of this class over the self-image of Americans. Ehrenreich also discusses the middle class's chronic "fear of falling," a fear of growing soft and losing discipline, leading to its retreat from responsible leadership in the society at large.

George Gallup, Jr. and Jim Castelli. The People's Religion: American Faith in the 90's. New York: Macmillan Publishing Co., 1989.

The result of years of research and polling people about faith, religious beliefs, ethical convictions, this is at once a portrait of Americans' religious life in the 1980's and a projection of the 1990's. Deeper spirituality surfaces as a desire of many Americans for the future.

William R. Hutchison, ed. Between the Times: The Travail of the Protestant Establishment in America, 1900-1960. New York: Cambridge University, 1989.

These essays focus on the dissolution of the Protestant establishment in terms of "cultural hegemony." The question is who is running the show. And the story is of how Protestant's lost the over-againstness with other groups that had constituted their own group identity, losing with it their influence in American society.

Wade Clark Roof and William McKinney. American Mainline Religion: Its Changing Shape and Future. New Brunswick and London: Rutgers University Press, 1987.

This is the book that sparked the ongoing conversation about shifts in America's religious landscape. Roof and McKinney document the decline of American "mainline" churches, the growth of evangelical churches, and the move of many Americans out of churches into the secular society.

Robert Wuthnow. The Restructuring of American Religion. Princeton: Princeton University Press, 1988.

Suggesting that World War II had the effect of drawing conservative and liberal Protestant toward the middle and that in the postwar era--prior to Vatican II--Protestants' major battles were waged with Roman Catholics, Wuthnow focuses on the present polarization of religious liberals and religious conservatives that runs through, not between the now-blurring boundaries between Protestant denominations. Observing that the liberal-conservative split was deepened between 1973 and 1980, Wuthnow concludes these constitute virtually separate religious communities.

Ministry

Richard Bondi. Leading God's People: Ethics for the Practice of Ministry. Nashville: Abingdon Press, 1989.

Weaving together stories of women and men in real-life situations, Bondi articulates a language for facing morally difficult pastoral situations and offers ethical reflection that avoids the temptation to easy answers. Indeed, the stories themselves exemplify the difference between "playing it safe" and exercising faithful leadership that is transformative.

Robert K. Greenleaf. Servant Leadership: A Journey Into the Nature of Legitimate Power and Greatness. New York: Paulist Press, 1977.

Addressing the current crisis of leadership in society at large, Greenleaf's main concern is for what seems to be indifference to the individual as servant and leader, as a person and in society. His breaths new life and meaning into the well-worn words, servant and leader, from his perspective that these are "mostly intuition-based concepts."

Lynn N. Rhodes. Co-Creating: A Feminist Vision of Ministry. Philadelphia: The Westminster Press, 1987.

In conversation with the thinking of feminist theologians and with practicing clergywomen, Rhodes articulates a vision of ministry that can be transformative for the whole church. She focuses on vital questions of authority, salvation, mission, and vocation.

Edward Schillebeeckx. The Church with a Human Face: A New and Expanded Theology of Ministry. New York: The Crossroad Publishing Co., 1985.

This book offers a socio-historical treatment of authority and leadership in the early church, as well as a discussion of the contemporary ciris of ministry. Schillebeeckx gives voice to the discontent among women, representing in his words "the most fundamental charge levelled at the churches." He also provides a critical assessment of two recent statements on ministry: the World Council of Churches' text, Baptism, Eucharist and Ministry, and the Vatican document, Sacerdotium Ministeriale.

Hans-Ruedi Weber. Living in the Image of Christ: The Laity in Ministry. Geneva: World Council of Churches, 1986.

Using the term "laity" to refer to those "who attempt to live as Christians both in the presence of God and in the midst of the world," Weber discusses the ministry of the laity as the human vocation, lived in the light of Christ. He takes up three worldwide human quests and considers how Christ responds to them: the human search for wisdom and the response of Christ the sage; the human cry for justice and Christ the crucified; the human need for identity and Christ the artist's restoration of God's image in us.

Ministry Formation

Sam Amirtham and S. Wesley Ariarajah, eds. Ministerial Formation in a Multifaith Milieu: Implications of Interfaith Dialogue for Theological Education. Geneva: World Council of Churches, 1986.

Based on the assumption that theological education and ministerial formation must both take place in context, this collection of papers addresses the reality that the context, in most parts of the world and increasingly in the United States, is one of religious pluralism. The collection focuses on the role ministers have in helping Christians grow in community with neighbors of other faith traditions.

Joseph C. Hough, Jr. and John B Cobb, Jr., eds. Christian Identity and Theological Education. Chico, CA.: Scholars Press, 1985.

A critique of current theological education that prepares leaders for white, middle-class North American churches, this book calls for a new understanding of Christian leadership: an understanding in which practical Christian thinking goes hand in hand with reflection in practice, and in which the global context of Christian life and work is engaged.

Joseph C. Hough, Jr. and Barbara G. Wheeler, eds. Beyond Clericalism: The Congregation as a Focus for Theological Education. Atlanta, GA.: Scholars Press, 1988.

This collection of papers in crafted as a response to James F. Hopewell's paper, "A Congregational Paradigm for Theological Education," in which he called for a paradigm shift for theological studies. Hopewell envisioned a new program for education that would move from a clerical paradigm, in which the individual is the focus of formation, to a congregational paradigm, in which the formation of the life and faith of the congregation is central. These papers offer various ecclesial and disciplinary perspectives on this proposed paradigm shift.

Maggie Ross. Pillars of Fire: Power, Priesthood, and Spiritual Maturity. San Francisco: Harper & Row, Publishers, 1988.

Ross challenges contemporary churches' understanding of ministry by making a compelling case that priesthood or ministry as a way of being and serving cannot be bestowed by ordination. She calls us back to our baptismal vows "to be on fire with the love of God . . . to radiate the light of the consuming fires of love" and says that those willing "to become such pillars of flame are the people to whom we should be looking for a way out of the current religious swamp."

The Mud Flower Collective. God's Fierce Whimsy: Christian Feminism and Theological Education. New York: The Pilgrim Press, 1985.

Written by seven women--black, hispanic, and white Christian women--who seek to practice what they preach, this is a testimonial to feminist commitment to change what violates the intellectual integrity of education. The integrity of this book is deepened as these women wrestle on paper with how difficult it can be to teach and learn together with minds set on justice.